BRUM

and

CANDLELIGHT

FRONT COVER PAINTING

SATURDAY NIGHT IN THE OLD BULL RING

By Robert K. Calvert

BRUM and CANDLELIGHT

A Walk Down Memory Lanes

by

MARY ELIZABETH SHOTT

foreword
by
Dr. Carl Chinn

Transcript & Book preparation
by: Maurice W. White

BREWIN BOOKS

First published by
Brewin Books, Studley, Warwickshire, B80 7LG
in 1995

Reprinted 1995

ISBN 1 85858 067 6

British Library Cataloguing in Publication Data
A Catalogue record for this book is available from the British Library

Typeset in Times by Avon Dataset Ltd, Bidford on Avon, Warks, B50 4JH

Printed in Great Britain by The Alden Press, Osney Mead, Oxford

Mary Elizabeth Shott

(MOM & OUR NAN)

1903 – 1990

• • • • • • • • • • • •

This book is Dedicated
to
My Children
and
My Grandchildren

• • • • • • • • • • • • •

Contents

•••••••••

Foreword

History belongs to everyone. But people seem to be wary about taking their rightful place in history. They feel that their lives are uninteresting. They believe that nothing much has happened to them. And they are convinced that they have not contributed to the making of history. They are wrong. Everyone's life is interesting. Something has happened to everyone. And every person has made history. Mary Elizabeth Shott knew this. She has written down her memories and she has shown clearly that she has played a part in the past. In the process she has made it plain that history cannot be owned by any one group. It includes everyone. That means those who were poor are as important in history as those who were well off.

Mary Elizabeth Shott grew up in a place that was renowned as one of the greatest manufacturing cities in the world. People poured into Birmingham looking for work and seeking a chance. They came from the surrounding villages of Warwickshire, Worcestershire and Staffordshire; they came from Wales and Scotland; they came from Ireland; they came from Italy; and they came from the Jewish area of the Russian Empire. Between 1821 and 1871, migration and natural increase meant that Birmingham's population expanded enormously from 106,000 to 343,000.

Many of these people were unskilled in manufacturing trades and they could afford only the cheapest and worst forms of housing. These were jerry-built back-to-backs. Erected in terraces with another row attached to their backs, they were separate from each other by a one-brick wall. They were tiny three-roomed structures, which had no running water. Lavatories were in a communal yard and were shared between two or more families; whilst each wash-house – brew'us – belonged to all the people who lived in a terrace. Rubbish was placed in battered miskins – brick-built outhouses. Because they were insanitary and unhealthy, the building of further back-to-backs was banned by a local bye-law in 1876. Still there were over 43,000 of them in 1914, and during the inter-war years 200,000 Brummies lived in these decrepit and outdated properties.

Indeed as late as 1960 there remained over 20,000 back-to-backs in Birmingham. The last of them were lived in until 1971.

It was in one of these house that Mary Elizabeth Shott was born, in the district of Digbeth. Later her family moved a short distance, into the adjoining area of Deritend. Lying in the valley of the River Rea, these two localities were the core around which Birmingham developed. Yet most of it's people did not share in the growing wealth of the city. As 'Our Nan' states "we the full blooded Brummie all shared one common enemy. His name was known as 'Poverty' ". Poor but proud, the people of Digbeth and Deritend were amongst the hundreds of thousands who laboured and created things and who turned Birmingham into the workshop of the world. Exempt from the fruits of their hard work, they built strong communities. Here, in their own ends, they fought poverty with dignity and determination. And they strove to make a better society for their children.

Mary Elizabeth Shott brings alive the vitality, the sharing and the pride of the poor of Brum. She shows their importance and she asserts their significance. A well-loved mom and nan, Mary Elizabeth Shott has all the skills of a story teller. She has had the confidence to tell her life in her own words. In that way she has claimed a place in history not just for herself, but also for all those who were touched by her presence.

Dr Carl Chinn, Community Historian
The University of Birmingham

Section One

Introduction
and
Farewell Letter

High Street, Deritend, 1903.
Photograph: Birmingham Central reference Library
Local Studies Section

High Street, Deritend, 1995

Introduction

Mary Elizabeth Shott, (Lizzie), at the age of sixteen years in 1920, was faced with a daunting future. Her father was lying in his coffin in an upstairs room, whilst her mother was nursing her eighth child, a ten day old girl. The day before the funeral, – well let us quote Lizzie:-

" . . . and on the Monday I went to get my Black, from Moor St. Warehouse. I kissed my Mom and baby sister, and said I would be back as soon as possible . . .". And on returning, " . . . When I entered our street from Deritend I knew something was wrong by the people gathered . . . by our house . . . My Mom had died in her sleep, and the baby was nestled in her arms . . .". The Doctor told her " . . . my Mom died of a broken heart . . . So now I had two coffins in this house, which I hated for ever after. I was frightened for the future for us all . . .".

There was worse to come, in the immediate aftermath of this trauma a younger brother and sister, both of whom were suffering from the same flu epidemic, which had taken their Father, were even then in Erdington Infirmary. Lizzie continues, "We had an inmate from the Infirmary, with a note to say my darling little Elsie had passed away, that's how you were informed in those so called, Good Old Days. It seemed my Mom and Dad called her to rest, one of their brood . . .". Not surprisingly Lizzie then continues . . . "I have now changed from a girl, who had known only love, even in deep poverty, to a frightened young woman . . .".

This is a story of Lizzie's early life, in and around Deritend, living originally in Fazeley Street, and later at the time of the above events in Alcester Street. It is not however a story, as Lizzie wrote it in the last year of her life, when in her eighty sixth year, as a walk down her 'Memory Lanes', as she called them. It was written for, and at the behest of her family, not just her married daughters and their children, but also for her own memories of her brothers and sisters, (and the latter is an amazing series of events). She involves her immediate family all along the line, with questions of morals, posers, and her beliefs. For me it is an amazing social document, with events ranging from the unbelievably cruel (Morally), to the highly humorous.

Only one month after completing it, Lizzie passed away, greatly mourned by her much extended Family. And what an amazing surprise on opening their Christmas stockings the following year, fifteen copies of "Our Nan's" hand written manuscript were to be found, one for each member of that family.

No printed manuscript such as this can ever replace Nan's original. It has of course been necessary to introduce Paragraphs for clarity, however the text has not been altered in any way. Essential, was the keeping of Nan's "Brummie accent", by which I mean I have retained Nan's spelling in certain areas. In particular, her 'were' for 'where'; 'as' for 'has', and I love to hear her 'done' for 'did'. With regard to the spelling of proper Names, it is more difficult. At one point Nan refers to "Ernie Mcguloch", the famous character (Brum' wise, that is) from the Bull Ring. This was of course Ernie McCulloch, you will see for yourselves why this should not be changed. There are one or two others, but I will take only one more, to hopefully avoid any family confusion. Nan's brother Charlie, plays, as do all the others, a very important part in her life, and she uses the spelling 'Charly' and 'Charley', apparently as an endearment. As she also uses Charlie, I have used the latter form through-out.

I feel most privileged and humble, to have been given the opportunity of reading, Nan's life. I do thank you, all the family, but Mrs Jean Bishop in particular for allowing this, my intrusion. I do hope that future readers will get from it, the Wisdom of "Our Nan", and so be enriched by her love for her family, neighbours and friends. Her love in-fact for people, not the material things of life, of which she had so little, in her life.

I am sure that this would be "Mom & Our Nan's" wish.

Thankyou
Maurice W. White

July 14' 1988

To
My Wonderful family
....
I want to thank
each one, of you for the
love and kindness you
have <u>all</u> given me.
It has kept me going
through all the years
which at times had not
been easy. I hope with all
'my heart' that your love and
concern for each other will
always last. What ever befalls
any of you my Spirit will
be watching over you and
guiding you. "God Bless" and
Take Care Of You.

Mom & Our Nan
XXX
XX

*This was not part of "Our nan's" story,
but was found later as a Farewell letter*

The Infant Lizzie
with her Father and Mother
Alfred and Annie Shott
c 1905

a Studio photograph of Lizzie
– her growing up years –
c 1921

Section Two

Nan's Narrative

1903 — 1989

Brum and Candlelight

My family want to walk with me,
down memory lane, it's 85 yrs
long, with quite a lot of streets and
roads leading off it.
It began for me in 1903, in a street
called Allison St a very poor part
of Brum, in a ~~district~~ district called
~~Deritend~~ Digbeth. My memories came to life
in 1904, when we then lived in a
street called Fazely street, same
old district. That was the year I
started to go to school and my
fondest memories began. The school
stills stands, and in my mind a
wonderful Monument to "Dear Old Brum"
No finer teachers or more respected,
ever controlled a class of poor
bare footed kids. When you take a
walk down Floodgate or Milk St
you see her boldly standing there.

Page 1 of Nan's Original Narrative

10

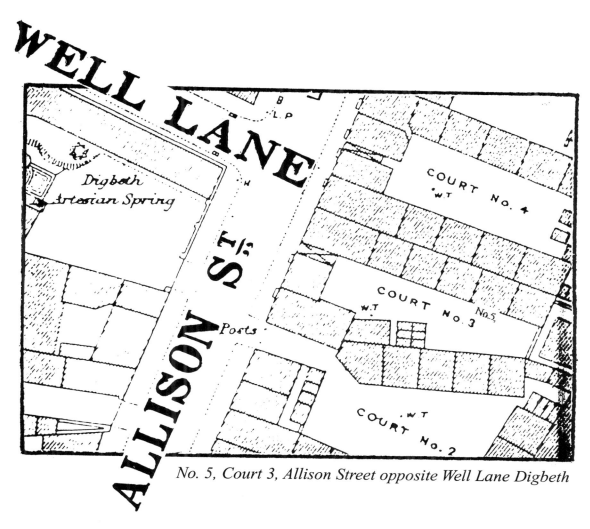

No. 5, Court 3, Allison Street opposite Well Lane Digbeth

Digbeth Police Station 1995

2

During the second "World War" Hitler rained his bombs, but she defied him even though many people died. The first War did not harm our "beloved Brum" very much, as regards buildings but took an awful toll of her sons. I remember young soldiers coming to see their teachers before going off to France and so very many not coming back. Brum gave her share of heroes from the "Warwicks" as our own Regiment was known. "Memory Lanes", all have a quota of rain and sunshine, tears and laughter. When I look back I marvel at the changes that have taken place in my life time. They are good or bad, which way you look at most changes, and acept them. I dont like the concrete blocks of buildings, they have taken away the character of this wonderful, Old City, and still doing so. I recall a walk or

Page 2 of Nan's Original Narrative

1903–1989

Brum and Candlelight

My family want to walk with me, down memory lane, it's 85 yrs long, with quite a lot of streets and roads leading off it.

It began for me in 1903, in a street called Allison St. a very poor part of Brum, in a district called Digbeth. My memories came to life in 1907, when we then lived in a street called Fazeley street, same old district. That was the year I started to go to school and my fondest memories began. The school still stands, and in my mind a wonderful monument to "Dear Old Brum". No finer teachers, or more respected, ever controlled a class of poor bare footed kids. When you take a walk down Floodgate or Milk St. you see her boldly standing there.

During the second "World War" Hitler rained his bombs, but she defied him even though many people died. The first war did not harm our "beloved Brum" very much, as regards buildings but took an awful toll of her Sons. I remember young soldiers coming to see their teachers before going off to France and so very many not coming back. Brum gave her share of heroes from the "Warwicks" as our own Regiment was known.

"Memory Lanes", all have a quota of rain and sunshine, tears and laughter. When I look back I marvel at the changes that have taken place in my life time. They are good or bad, which way you look at most changes, and accept them. I don't like the concrete blocks of buildings, they have taken away the character of this wonderful "Old City", and still doing so.

I recall a walk or tram ride, a penny fare would take you along Fazeley St, or through Bordesley and Deritend to High St and along Moor St and into the City. I found it an enchanting world as a child all the lovely shops, not stores, and "barrow boys", also Farmers, shouting out loud their wares, in the "Bull Ring". We had a grand "Market Hall" but War did rob us of that treasure. It was full of stalls selling wonderful goodies. I loved Jenkin's with its Machine making all kinds of sweets, Oh those Mouth Watering "Fishes". Then on Sat. night I went with my Mom and Dad, because that's when you got your bargains. The Fish and Meat was auctioned off, we had no fridges, in that long ago, and so it was sold off cheaply, rather than thrown away.

When you came out again into the Bull Ring the stalls were lit by flares, and I see the vendors swinging them round and round to get them working, gas and electric came much later. I can see Rabbits and Fowl hanging from all the stands and lovely large eggs on show. Everything was so fresh and cheap, but its silly to compare with today. We talked in pennies not pounds, only I doubt whether people who have passed on, could have enjoyed the plenty of today in "Brum".

13

We had a Meat Market in Jamaica Row and the Meat was almost thrown at you on Sat. night. But also we had a very good class of butcher by the name of Shorthouse, only the "Shambles" was more popular because of the prices. We had a shop on the corner of Edgbaston St, Pearks by name and sixpence would get you one and a half pound of Margarine. We had quite a few shops going along the row to the "Bull Ring", shoes hanging outside the doors selling from 1/11pence a pair. If you reached New St, many high class shops selling nice things, as we called them.

Sir Smedley Crooke owned a Jewellery shop, which was also a Pawn shop. When the lads came back from War and to a terrible depression, quite a few medals were on show for sale in those windows. The "Boer War" was still talked about in those days, and we never dreamt of the horrors of those yet to come.

We the full blooded Brummie all shared one common enemy his name was known as "Poverty". I called his offspring pubs and pawnshops. What tales could be told about both. But our Bull Ring belonged to us , and it's hard to describe how very much alive it was always. Lord Nelson looked down on everything that was going on and saw quite a lot even with that one eye. Sunday was the only day when shops closed, and the Talent came to life. Preachers in plenty shouting each other down, one regular was always on his box every Sunday night. I remember listening to him amidst crowds of people, who would maybe argue with him and nearly always come off second best.

No such word as mugging in those days, and which is really "highway robbery" with violence and should be treated as such. Oh yes we all loved Ernie Mcgulock-(near enough) he done quite a lot of good work for the poor with his pal Mr Pentland. We will come back down the Bull Ring and pass Park street, along which were many houses, and a lodging house or doss house as they were called in those days. There was a picture house also, bearing in mind we only had silent films and in some halls, like "Digbeth Institute", Magic Lanterns.

It is easy to overlook old fashioned shops in my memory but we had hot pies just below Park street, and lovely Pork pies made in a very old fashioned shop below St Martin's Church, name of Tabberner. I should have mentioned Hurrells the bacon shop just before we reached New St, and who sold us a large bag of bacon pieces on Saturday morning for sixpence, must get on spot early. We also had another treat from the cake shop just after we reached Park St named Godfree, a big bag of stale cakes for sixpence. In those days I don't think we realized we were poor, it was a way of life, and we just got on with it. I spent half my life in Deritend and learned a lot of lessons, mostly the meaning of the strength of character.

We will walk down "Heath Mill Lane" still there, and the very Old Pub on the corner "Old Crown". A few yards down the lane lived a Lady, in my mind a real one. She went by the name of Nurse Tucker. Into the world she brought

Floodgate Street School
'. . .the Best School in Brum . . .'

Heath Mill Lane
Old Library and News-Rooms

The Old Crown, Deritend

Nurse Tuckers house 1995
No. 17 Heath Mill Lane

hundreds of pedigree babies, by which I mean Brummies, because in those far off days we had few overseas visitors, (no slur intended). You do well to compare "then and now" in her field of work. The working hours never known, it could be day or night, she was always on call, and her Cloak, easier than a coat to put on, and a black bag, always at the ready.

We will take a night call, say eleven thirty, and if baby was good, maybe arrived about 4 or 5 o'clock in the small hours. She stayed until all was safe to leave, but how she worked during those hours, and so often under terrible conditions. Dad was sent away, after fetching Nurse and carrying black bag, no cars in days of long ago. The rest of the kids (if any) tucked away behind closed doors. The fire was well stoked up, because a lot of hot water was needed, and bear in mind all had to be carried upstairs. Then all was clear and quiet if baby decided that way, then nurse departed for a few hours. But she came back at around ten or maybe a little later in the morning. Mother and baby inspected, and the rest left to a kindly neighbour. This ritual went on for ten days, when Mom could get up and take charge.

My tears come at this stage, because I see myself carrying up a bowl of water, soap and towels and helping my Mom wash the younger ones. Our kind neighbours "God Bless" them all, had their own families to look after. The nurse for all this hard work received, if lucky, thirty shillings, sometimes got by a few shillings weekly. When Lloyd George brought about insurance laws it rose to two pounds. When you compare this instance with today's dealing with babies, how thankful we should all be.

Now just a little further down the lane close to Nurse Tucker was the Blacksmith, and as a girl I loved to see him shape the horseshoes and put on the horses feet. Oh those beautiful hard working horses, where did they all go, lost in the name of progress. Across the road facing Armstrong the blacksmith, right name strangely enough for the job, we had the basket maker. Mr Preedy could be seen any time of day sitting on the floor of his premises, weaving cane. He made all kinds of articles mostly carriages put on wheels. These were let out on hire, a small deposit and sixpence an hour. A bit more of a Brummie life, his transport, and all he could afford. I went early along with many more, from around Deritend on Sat. mornings, to get a decent carriage to get coke. We queued for ages at times with large sugar sacks, the bigger the better. The coke wharf was on corner of Glover St. down Adderley St. next opening from Heath Mill Lane, we hoped for a kind hearted man to serve us, who weighed the coke on very large scoop like scales and mostly didn't bother about weight, but just filled our bags as full as was possible. If "Candid Camera" had been around in those days they would have had a field day. We used all kinds of takeaways, old prams, carts of any shape or size. If one broke down, they always found helping hands, that's how really good Brummies always behave.

Well I must get back to Heath Mill Lane, I've got off my Memory Lane which I was afraid I'd do. A bit further along the lane was, Wheatley's the undertaker on corner of Trinity St, the building is still there. He was a very busy man most of the time. I have seen whole families wiped out with T.B. and thanked God, when it was got under control. There were hundreds of houses in and around this quarter, terraces with back to back houses. We shared lavatories and wash houses, may be that's why we were called big hearted "Brummies", we had to share, got no choice. I take you right along this lane, and we pass a little sweet shop, converted house, really, everything was home made. A little barrel was on the counter and when I spent my half penny I always prayed it was full because it got me an egg cup full of lovely peppermint. When we reach the corner what do we find? a Pawnshop and on the opposite side, on the corner of Great Barr Street, the public house called the "Forge Tavern", while "Mother Poverty" looks proudly on.

When I was a little girl I would gaze into "Marrions" window, name of the owner. She had one window in Heath Mill Lane, and another in Fazeley St. I loved the one in Fazeley St, it was full of rings, watches etc, and I hoped that one day I would own a wrist watch even though they were terribly big in those days. Now next door still in Fazeley Street, was a very nice Coffee Shop, it was very clean, called "Deeley's" coffee house. We had not heard the word "Cafe" in those days. We'll pop inside, always welcome and did not need many coppers. In those far off days nearly all public places had one thing in common, sawdust on the floor, whether boards or shining red tiles. We got a good sized glass of hot tea, half milk, and you get a lovely dough nut or dripping cake, if I remember right two or three pence would cover the cost.

It was not very large inside, and you sat on well scrubbed benches with the same kind of table. When it was cold weather, a bright shining fire was laid on. The customers did not stay long, they were mostly Carters, who had loaded the carts, from the busy wharf and factories. We had not got around to Canteens in those days and so we had many coffee shops dotted around, but very few as nice as "Deeley's", my opinion of course.

If I stay a few minutes we can go over the bridge of Great Barr St. On the crest of the bridge was a bake house name of "Wilson". Every Cottage loaf was weighed as you bought it. I liked it to be short of it's two pounds, because then you got what was called "make weight" and if you were lucky, it was a dripping or Chelsea bun. This is another big contrast of today, when cakes are selling at around fifty 'p', which makes it ten shilling in old money. But we must remember if a man got two pounds in his weekly pay-packet, he had a good job and today a child at school 'gets' that much or more.

I don't like a lot of the changes that have taken place but most of them have

Site of '... Nan's Coke Wharf...'
Adderley Street/New Bond Street

Site of Wheatley's ... Funeral Director ...
Heath Mill Lane/Lower Trinity Street

The Forge Tavern
Fazeley Street/Great Barr Street

. . . Whilst on the opposite side . . .
. . . Mother Poverty looks proudly on . . .
Deeley's Coffee House being next door

20

made life easier for us "Old Uns". I had a wonderful Mom and Dad, and know how they went without themselves to give us, as our family got bigger, and no more money to cope with the situation. We lived in a back house in Fazeley street and we shared a large yard, I think there were twelve or maybe fourteen houses. We had a large lamp in centre of yard, and it was visited each night by our lamp lighter who carried a large pole over his shoulder. It was grand to see him reach up and lighten our darkness, we could then play skipping and hopscotch, while the lads argued over a game of marbles. We had two wash houses and six lavatories, and made your own arrangement how you shared them. A large tap was outside, the water was carried indoors as you needed it, a very cold job in the winter months. We were all in trouble when the tap froze, but like most of our problems we shared, and willing hands poured hot water over the tap, and laughed when water gushed out once more.

Everything was kept clean and as children we were told to help by being tidy and learning how to use a broom. It was not very hard to do all these things, because our houses were small, one living room, and may be one bedroom and an attic, but we always managed. We were not spoilt for choice like we are today, but I must confess we could nearly always move on. The rent of houses varied by size and locality, and you could see the sign "This house to let" in the window of an empty dwelling. The name of the deputy was on the notice, and she held the key for you to enter and look it over. If you decided it, to rent was what you required, you paid her, usually it was a shilling, and the house was yours.

When we look back down our lanes of memory so much as changed, we can hardly believe it. We had lamps hanging from the ceiling or a table lamp, but in the bedroom we nearly all relied on candles. I doubt you could go into a house and find it without candles, they were cheap by today's standards, maybe one shilling a bundle or one halfpenny each.

We had so many factories on the Fazeley street area I wonder why people were so poor. Every trade was around, that you could mention. Heavy stampings, hammers banging out products, day and night at the Deritend stamping, in Liverpool street, Rolling mills, nuts & bolts, tinsmiths, foundries etc, where as it all gone? We had Fellows, Morton & Clayton, the name is still showing as large as life, and I recall the Boaties as they were known. The women with large bonnets with a kind of cape around the neck, and rows of beads, the men had earrings, sleepers, as known then, but the only men to wear such things in those days. These men and women were as strong as the horses that they led along the canal paths. The loads were very heavy because of the goods loaded on the barges.

We had very few cars in the days I'm talking about. When you walked up Fazeley street you came upon the Italian quarter, and along Andover street, they were all busy making "Ice Cream". It was transported in lovely little colourful carts, and would stop any place they found a customer, they made delicious ice cream, and a halfpenny would buy you a cornet, and one penny a pie. They were not large but so mouth watering and I wonder how they got a living, but then we were easy to please, just jogging along life's highway.

We also had on the corner our very own doctor Murphy, by name and as Irish as they came. He was loved by all in the district and often a wee bit tiddly, but for one shilling we got his advice, and a bottle of medicine. I remember that every house in those days had its own medicine shelf composed mostly from herbs. The summers (yes we had them in those days too) found a bowl of Brimstone & treacle black, on every table, and Mom made sure we had a large spoon-ful. The winters found us indulging in lovely hot stews, plenty of fresh veg's and creamy spuds. I wonder what harm as been done to us today with all the fancy meals and Freezers. Oh well its just my opinion and I know we must move on all the time, but food mountains make me angry with so much starvation in the world.

Well before I leave Fazeley St. I must say I was joined by a brother, (Our Bill), Alfred William really, and a sister Annie. They were both christened at "Pipes Mission" on the corner of Floodgate St, the building still stands but now part (or was) of a factory, the original windows looking like stained glass, still shining. In those days boys were dressed like little girls in plaid frocks, but not pinafores. When they reached age five years they were what was called Breeched and that meant put into short trousers with pockets in. He was taken around always on a Sunday, to neighbours and relatives and money put into the pockets. It was one of those little things of the past that to me is a treasured memory simple and lovely.

We also had a little Church just around the corner in Heath Mill Lane, "St.Basil's" by name and it was full on Sunday morning and evening . I think we must have been more "God Fearing" in those days. It is still there and used as a shelter for homeless boys which sadly are very many. By this time our family was too large for our little house and talk of a move was going on. I look back now and think only of Love and kindness in my first memories of my life and with so little of the worlds goods that we all seem to have today.

My dad got another job at this time, in Small Heath at Alldays & Onions, and we moved to a nice terrace house opposite the works, it was so easy to find another house in those days if you could afford 5 to 7 shillings a week. We must always remember that was a good slice out of a man's weekly wage. I left my beloved school and went to Montgomery St. I suppose it was alright, I did get a prize which were given out in those days for attendance and good behaviour. I don't hold many memories of that school but I do of the house

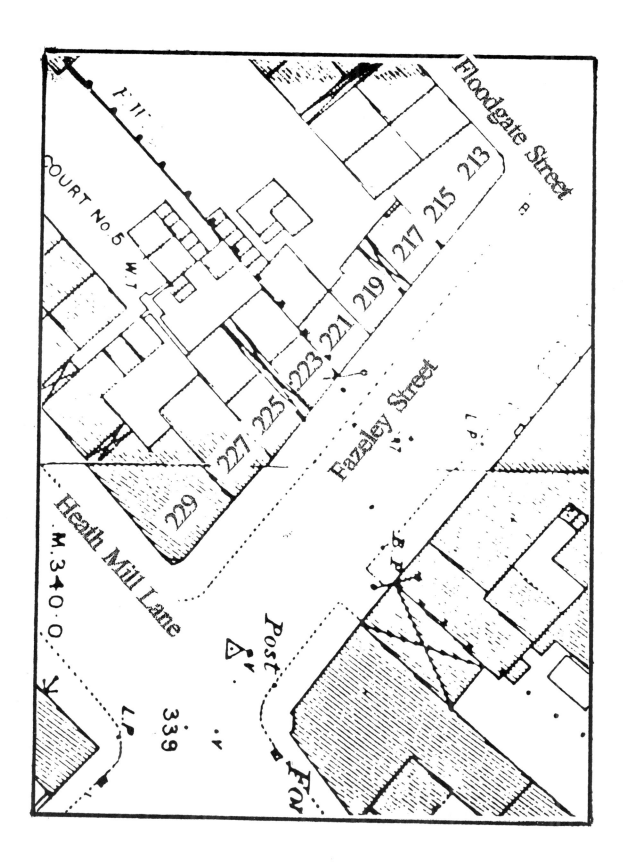

Original Shops and Houses 1889
: 229 : 227 : 225 : 223 : 221 : 219 ; 217 ; 215 : 213 :
from Heath Mill Lane to Floodgate Street

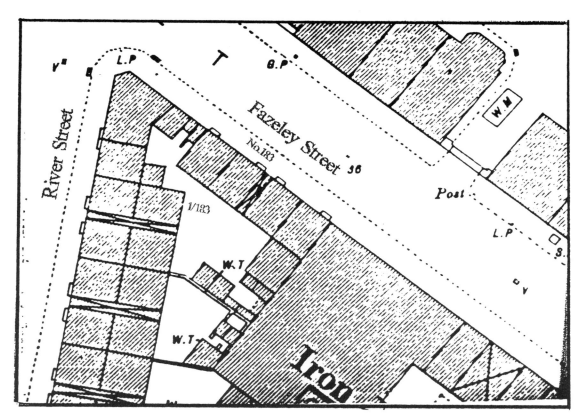

Back House 1/183, in court behind 183 Fazeley Street
corner with River Street

Site' Left 'No. 183 Fazeley Street and 1/183 in rear Court
behind fenced yard

'...those Boaties...as strong as their horses...'
the Canal Carriers

Back-to-Back houses
Floodgate Street/Fazeley Street

*** Nan's . . . 'Pipes Mission' . . .*
Floodgate Street/Fazeley Street
*** Note: this building was 'The Birmingham Free Christian Society Sunday School'*
that it is believed Nan refers to; but no confirmation has been found

The former 'St. Basils' Church'
Heath Mill Lane

Thomas Tudor: Picture Frame Maker c.1905
130/132/134 Heath Mill Lane
Photograph: Lance Tudor, permission for use given by Mrs L. Tudor

Site of the former Mr Tudor's shop 1995
the Centre double door still carries the No's 132 and 134 on the Transom

22

old irish couple living next door to us and he used to send me along to the "Marlborough Pub" on the corner of Anderton Rd for a pint of beer. I had to take a bottle, and a label was put across the cork. When Mr Costellow had drunk his beer he became very talkative and always demanded "Home Rule" for his beloved Ireland. This was my growing up stage I suppose and I learned that some people lived under better conditions than others. I remember seeing the 'Comet' in the sky and was realy afraid because other children told me if its tail touched the ground, it would be the end of the World. I should make a point here about the fears of children and how they can live in the mind for ever, and like love, create impressions. This was not a bad time for people I supose realy, we had a Coronation coming along and being young, it was all excitement, street parties and I remember my big paper hat.

and the people we lived by, both were very nice indeed.

We had two doors, back and front entrance, a parlour and our very own toilet, and a copper which enabled my Mom to wash the clothes when she liked. We had our own back garden to dry the washing, instead of sharing a large open yard. My Gran lived with us, 'Dads' Mom and did so until she was eighty five, I suppose my Grandad must have died and she came to us. She went to work at a warehouse in Edgbaston Street, to me she was an Old lady, always sitting in her rocking chair. But she did bring me some very lovely dolls, and train sets for my brother, from were she worked.

The pubs opened at six o'clock in the morning and all day until eleven o'clock at night. We had a dear old Irish couple living next door to us, and he used to send me along to the "Marlborough Pub" on the corner of Anderton Rd. for a pint of beer. I had to take a bottle, and a label was put across the cork. When Mr. Costellow had drunk his beer he became very talkative and always demanded "Home Rule" for his beloved Ireland. This was my growing up stage I suppose and I learned that some people lived under better conditions than others. I remember seeing the "Comet" in the sky and was really afraid because other children told me if it's tail touched the ground, it would be the end of the World. I should make a point here about the fears of children and how they can live in the mind for ever, and like love, create impressions. This was not a bad time for people I suppose really, we had a Coronation coming along and being young, it was all excitement, street parties and I remember my big paper hat.

When you are young you don't understand anything about being rich or poor but the quality of home life most certainly affects your future life, in my opinion. I got much joy at this time, by going to Small Heath park and often lovely bands played in the stand and Pierrots entertained. I could also make daisy chains, sitting in the fields that later became the B.S.A. factory, which was already at end of Armoury Rd. It was a busy works, making bikes and needles and rifles, and how terribly sad to think part of it would become a tomb for many of its workers in the years to come, when the second awful War came.

I don't know the reason why we left this lovely little house and returned to Deritend, but maybe fate does play a big part in all our lives, and things happen which we have no control over. I remember at this time there were grand large houses all around this area, sadly all gone now, as years take their toll every where. We moved back to Deritend and I went back to my beloved school in Floodgate St, our family had started to grow by this time, and I had another sister. I knew nothing about how babies arrived, such things were not talked about in those days, it seemed to me that every house had their fare share or very often more so.

* * *

29

A lot of things were happening at this time , it was wonderful to see and hear the first Gramophone, much better than the phonograph. Then we had such a lot of artistes on the Music Halls and even I remember quite a few. "Lily of Laguna" was sung in every house and then came "Alexanders Rag Time band". Then Mrs Pankhurst was on every one's lips, and she and her group of followers, did at last get us ladies the vote, but they fought long and hard, for what we enjoy today. I think troubles had started by now, but one didn't hear so early about them as we do now, Mines had more tragedies and lives lost, and we lost poor Captain Scott, a very brave man.

I knew poverty was very much now around, as at my school, cocoa and thick hunks of bread and jam were given out in the mornings. We also had shower baths, which I thought were great, boys came to school bare footed, and our mothers washed some of our clothing out over night and dried by the fire for the next day. We could still put a long skipping rope across our streets and anyone could join in, which young ladies going to work often did. This was a bit of pleasure that cost nothing and quite a few girls who worked at Birds Custard and the A.C.Sphinx would jump into the rope. The traffic was very light these days and trams were only on the Main Roads, a few horse drawn carts on the side streets. We had the milk man who pushed his cart and would stop to serve you a penny worth of creamy milk, and the hawkers who pushed an hand cart, selling Rabbits at six pence or larger one for ninepence. It was possible to buy a lovely oily pair of Macduff kippers for tuppence or a nice smoked bloater.

We have come such a long way in our eating habits, but I wonder if its all good, these drastic changes. We nearly all cooked by an open fire, and however poor, a joint on Sunday was a must, and open doors proved it by the lovely smells. In those far off days children could work half time if they liked, I did because what little I earned helped to buy my clothes, and so did most of my school friends. I went to a factory and helped to assemble small tin toys and got two and sixpence or may be three shillings a week, I loved it and felt quite grown up. We didn't get home work from school but you certainly had to do your lessons, or else, while in your class. I loved my school and was taught such a lot that as helped me through life.

We had mixed classes, and were not saints by any means, one never heard the word "Sex" it was just something what told us Male or Female. We had to obey rules and respect them, also to have self respect and accept discipline. There were only a few children who did not conform as most Parents went along with the teachers. Every teacher had a "Cane" but seldom used it, and if you got a couple of strokes on your hands, you got no sympathy at home as your parents, knew you deserved it. You were graded from standard one to seven x, I went from standard five to seven, and I stayed in this class until I left school at fourteen years old, which was leaving age, no matter what class, you had reached by then.

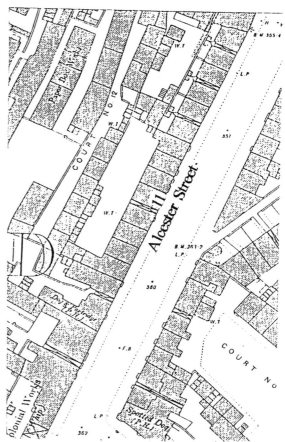

No. 11 Alcester Street
rear court access through one entry only
used by the eight properties

Nan's three daughters standing outside the site of 11 Alcester Street
all three of whom were born in the house

people, mostly all, who lived in Deritend and, working districts of "Dear Old Brum". My school, as I always call it, did get us a few treats, Mr Pentland came on a visit and brought "Family Tickets" for a "Ragged Robins" outing, only a "Tram Ride" starting from Severn Street. We were taken to Ufculme Park, to us kids, it seemed miles away and what a thrill, to recieve a bag of goodies, buns and fruit, We sang all the way there on our "stream of tram cars and I doubt any child of today even riding in a "Rolls" and enjoyed such a day out. I do wonder how many of my old school friends are left to recall all these Bye gone years. There were three of us called the "dauntless three", and I know one as passed away a couple of years back, It is worth remembering her, a good true Blue Brommie of long ago. She went to work every morning at six o'clock in the "wholesale fruit & veg: market marcket and still reached school at nine o'clock, She was one of ten children and very poor, but also respectable like most

Page 29 of Nan's Original Narrative

This is the lane where I am meandering, because so much springs to my mind from my casket of memories. We have changed the face of the globe so much over the last sixty years, that all our hard working teachers seem to have taught in vain. Countries have been swallowed up, currency changed and twelve times table disappeared. The English language mutilated and slang as taken it's place, so that it is a real pleasure to hear it spoken, as it should be.

I am a "Brummie" and talk like one, and also proud of the fact, but don't have to use slang words. I am remembering a lot, those teachers of long ago tried to instil into our Grey matter as they called the substance between our ears. I am astounded that boys and girls leave school these days, and knowing so little about normal life. My generation had so very little of worldly goods and it makes me realize what an asset it really was. We valued every extra that came our way, and counted as a bonus, all that today, we seem to demand as our right. In this lane I am getting older and know, that with a bigger family we are poor, like all the people, mostly all, who lived in Deritend and, working districts of "Dear Old Brum". My school as I always call it, did get us a few treats, Mr. Pentland came on a visit and brought Party Tickets for a "Ragged Robins" outing, only a Tram Ride starting from Severn Street. We were then taken to Uffculme Park, to us kids, it seemed miles away and what a thrill, to receive a bag of goodies, buns and fruit. We sang all the way there on our stream of Tram Cars and I doubt any child of today even riding in a "Rolls" enjoyed such a day out.

I do wonder how many of my old school friends are left to recall all these bygone years. There were three of us called the "Dauntless Three" and I know one as passed away a couple of years back. It is worth remembering her, a good true blue Brummie of long ago. She went to work every morning at six o'clock in the wholesale fruit & veg. market and still reached school at nine o'clock. She was one of ten children and very poor, but also respectable like most of us and her mom did own a very large "Mangle", with that family she did need it, and I swear it took ten minutes to turn the handle. Oh what joy our Mothers would have had with just a few of today's household tools. Thinking of this memory gives me another, a daring little group of us I expect us dauntless three thought this one up, we bought a penny packet of woodbines five cig's, and we all bravely tried smoking them in the school toilets. This clever deed made us all ill and we dare not tell the teacher why, it made her think she had an epidemic on her hands. This school friend and myself remained friends in our after years, and she got her reward for all her hardship, by owning her own fruit shops and a happy comfortable marriage. She was a success story, one of many, for Floodgate Street school and the poor quarter of Brum.

Well this part of my lane as been of my early memories of my part of dear old Brum, and I could recall quite a lot of incidents, but enough is enough, I hear my family saying, so will go further along the lane. It is hard not to wander a little because one thought, brings back other memories. I am getting older and ready to leave school, and that made me sad because with all the hardships we were a happy gang of kids. I am certain of one thing for sure, a large family meant more poverty and worry for our parents. We never had any handouts like today, no family allowance, nothing, only Granny got her old age pension seven and sixpence a week, and the old saying was "never mind half a loaf is better than none". My dad used to mend our boots, working on an iron foot sunk into a wooden log and then a better one was invented with three sizes and more shoes got mended. I used to go to a small old fashioned shop down Digbeth for sixpenny worth of pieces of leather and two penny worth of three quarter inch sprigs. My dad done a wonderful job to keep our feet dry and warm, but my eldest brother nearly always wore clogs they were cheap and lasted longer than boots, costing nine pence or one shilling a pair.

It is almost unbelievable when I compare then and today's standard of living, this in a City that made anything from a pin to a train. My opinion won't let me say they were good Old Days. I only wish those wonderful parents like mine, could have had a share of today's goodies. I wonder, now am I wrong? because we seem to have lost as much as we've gained. There seems more greed, but it seems to be needed to get a footing on life's ladder today. I have more brothers and sisters and that means we are getting poorer, and more worry on my mom and dads face. We still have lots of love the kind money will never ever buy, and I hope you all heed this and spread it amongst your own families, because it brings its own reward and as nothing to do with the worlds goods. I had my share of second hand clothes, the best my mom could afford, and we were all in the same boat and never ashamed, because poverty was no disgrace and not our fault.

We did not go to the pawnshop or strap shop as the small hucksters was called, who sold everything from a farthing candle to a halfpenny bundle of wood. My dad said you paid through the nose and it kept you poor, my God we were all poor in Deritend in those days. We had halfpenny packets of 'blacking' and two brushes and a piece of old velvet that was used on our boots every night ready for the next day, oh my didn't they shine. I used to fetch three penny worth of tea in a large jug on Sunday morning and we kids all clambered on Mom's bed, and it was shared, now you pay up to fifty pence for a cup and when I look back, it doesn't taste so nice, how could it?

I must start to move or this lane will never end and it was a bit crowded with the finest people I have ever met, big hearted mostly honest Brummies, the like will never be seen again. War clouds are gathering and tempers rising against Non British people, the biggest tragedy of War, friends become enemies overnight. Well, my family you asked for it and I told you the lane was long, and when my Great grand children read it, they will realize what a lot of changes can come in a life time. I neither condone or condemn because all Generations have problems, and could be solved by less greed, and more common sense.

But this is my lane and I have promised to tell you how I travelled along it, I want to keep it tidy, which brings to mind how untidy or worse we Brummies have become. This again starts in the home mostly, never mind how poor. At the early age of four or five, little girls owned a broom, one like Mom had, and taught how to use it in play, always a good way to learn. The pity today brooms are seldom used, the vacuum as taken over and just a touch of a button does the job. This day and age sees nearly everything is done the easy way, but have we lost interest and pride? We nearly all lived in a house that opened onto a street, so we looked on that bit outside our door as our bit of patch. Well that gave us the right to keep it clean and we did just that, swept outside everyday and buckets of water swilled also. It was woe betide the youngsters who threw paper down or wrote on the walls with chalk. This is were you escuse my spelling, my teacher of long ago, would have said a few words about it, and no escuses. I did go to the best school in Brum and the teachers done a wonderful job, but we did not always listen, (I was one). I ask myself is this one of the reasons for today's litter bugs and another one being, more wrappings on more goods.

The time I am writing about we had less money to buy like we do today, and children only got a few sweets served mostly from a jar and wrapped in a small cone shaped bag or even a piece of clean newspaper and I have told you we would not dare to throw it on the floor. We used to have men sweeping the roads and a horse drawn cart walking along aside them into which was thrown the rubbish. Then we also had a water cart which all boys and girls loved to follow behind, it was like a long shower and washed our roads, at times the driver put on more pressure and soaked us, but did not please Mom. I am going very slow along this part of my lane, because I am getting older and my childhood slipping away, but I am sure we did remain as children longer than today. We girls could sit on the edge of the gutter, and watch boys rolling marbles along the road, playing tip cat or running with a wooden or metal bowl. If we teased them we were chased and nearly always enjoyed being caught, as you would my lovely grand daughters, if you got such very nice kisses.

This was one aspect (word reborn) of our lives, pleasure that did not cost money and was so innocent to all us kids. But we did all grow up, and most of our young shoulders tried to take some of the load our parents were carrying, a case of every little helps. For myself I learned how to fill the hanging lamp with paraffin, clean the globe chimney and get the wick just right for lighting, put candles in safe place when alight. This was one job I did not like, but it had to be done to lighten our darkness, and I did envy any one who had gas in the home. I also new how to build and maintain a glowing fire, because that was our means of hot water and cooking, and I thanked God I did know how to cope with such things in the years to come.

I think I can move along my lane now, even though I could quote so much more. Well I will reach to 1914, what a terrible black wicked never to be forgotten year that became. I must have been eleven years old now, and still trying to enjoy school days, that were being marred by War talk and I could not understand why any men from any country wished to kill each other. My dad went, many relations and even boys I went to school with, after a time, because it seems we were short of man power. I wonder now very often, did we lose the cream of our manhood at this terrible time. When I left school at fourteen years old I went to work in the foundry same works as my dad, they were on War Work and I think every one else was at this time. I learned a trade which was a big help to me later on in years, and I loved it, but not the War part bit it made me so sad. I saw many wounded soldiers return home some without limbs or blinded or frost bitten, Oh "Dear God" I kept asking myself and I still do, Why?

When a soldier got a short leave, we decorated the street, it was no problem to put streamers across from one side to the other. What brave men they were, and all for a shilling a day. We at home got a few shocks also when German Zep's came over, no warnings given, only policemen on bikes calling out in the streets. The cry was "lights out zep's are over" and we all had Black or very dark Green paper blinds so it was easy to shut our poor lighting of this time. I was caught once when they came over, I had gone to Aston Hippodrome with a Dutch girl who had come here with her family, who worked in glass blowing in Deritend. We had to walk home and not one glimmer of light could be seen until we reached our Bull Ring. It was a faint glow showing an hole in the road were men had been working, but we made it at last and relieved our parents fears. I recall how every one was eager to do their bit in this terrible War, and women from all classes done jobs that no one would have thought possible a couple of years before. They delivered coal and swept the streets, worked on railways, and their heart never seemed good enough. So many of them gave all they held dear, at this terrible time, mothers, wives and sweethearts, and so very very young.

But all things have to end as did this war which was to end all wars. I was understanding by now, the meaning of sorrow and grief, it was written deep on the faces of all who had lost their loved ones. When the armistice was signed, party was held in all back streets and hopes born again but much misery was not far away. My home life was still good but getting no better off, money wise. I did get a lovely surprise one day, my dad bought me a second hand bike, I think it cost him four shillings, can you believe it?. I had a tin of Black enamel paint 6d =2½p, a new bell about the same price, a pair of mud guards 1/6 = 7½p and coloured laces that fitted through the guards, and my bike gave me more pleasure than a 'Rolls' can give anyone today. In my young years I went many miles on my bike, often with my dad who had a decent bike, and in this part of my journey back I am left with many tender memories.

I am telling you these incidents my children, so you can compare with things today. The word pleasure meant just that and today, with so much to possess it seems a dead word. I would tell you though we had many advantages in those days. We could cross our roads without fear, cars had not arrived and the lovely horses were in full control. It didn't seem to matter if you forgot to lock your house door, robbery was not rife like today, maybe it was because we had so little of much value or I like to think we cared more for each other as neighbours, than we do today.

Well if I leave the War behind, all the upsets it had bought, we did hope for much better times. It was not to be, men were in despair, broken in health and no were to turn to for help, no one to shout out loud for them in those days. The shortage of work was most acute and very bad even in my beloved Brum, we had been used to so many trades but the winds of change were blowing strongly. We had unbelievable hardships all around us, and I will quote you a few I hope please God you never witness. We had a lady called Sally Do-Da, named after a Music Hall song of the day. She walked along the street gutters singing "Count your Blessings" and was thrown coins from anyone who could spare a penny or halfpenny. It is so hard to believe, when a child of today receives an open cheque. Then we had another lady, I stand by calling them ladies because in my opinion that's what they all were. We had a poor soul who pushed a fairly large hand cart, selling Bricks of salt, we did not have packets in those days. We crushed it fine and put it into salt cellars on the table as we used pepper and mustard pots. My pantry shelves creaked with salt, how could you not buy off someone worse off than yourself. I tell you about these people so you can try and understand the terrible poverty of those days. Then on Friday nights a man pushed a Barrel organ along the streets and played in front of our houses, just a few coppers again was his reward, but we must remember twelve pennies make up to a shilling and that bought quite a lot of items in those days.

I am standing still in this part of my lane now, so many faces and people come to my mind, and every one could have wrote a book about their lives and without one word of fiction. We had a tall bony man with a little wife, he was called "Posh Price" and had been a Bare fisted boxer. They kept a small shop and I think five pounds would have bought his entire stock, he was scared of his tiny wife, funny really but true. One day as I remember, they just walked away and left all behind. We had a well known character known as "Tommy Tank", he must have been the first "Streaker" as I was told, doing it for a pint of beer. He would throw a brick through a pub window, and he had plenty of those around in Deritend and Digbeth. He was the first person on the black list and that meant he could not be served in any pub. I don't know where he was put, but I saw him when he was released, and he came to live with his sister, who lived close by me. He was then a quiet old man who earned a few shillings with a basket of dried fish on his arm.

I tell you these things my family, because of the vast changes that have taken place. Every Monday morning two ladies emerged from a side street, one of many incidents that could make you laugh or cry. They pushed and pulled a very large old pram, the contents were not babies, but piled up with bundles, on the way to the Pawn Shop. They worked on a commission I was told for the street, I won't give any names because they may have relatives still around. Well I must stop meandering along my lane because every household in it could have written a story about their full lives. They were all filled with people, and their goings on and not things, as we all had so little in that respect.

My love was still in my candle lit home, but I am sad to think what a struggle was going on in it, and how my parents must have gone short to feed and clothe us seven children. I think on looking back to nineteen, nineteen, this dear old England was completely changing. We had a very bad attack of Flu the aftermath of War I reckon and people were dying like flies, as the saying goes. This is were the price of War sickens me, men went to fight, quite young mostly, and those who came back (not many), looked old and tortured by what they had endured in four years of killing and being killed. I hate War it changed an whole Nation, nothing as ever been the same, well that's what your Nan thinks.

I am sixteen years old now, at this time, and my eldest brother nearly fifteen, I still worked in the foundry, but mostly on a short hours week, my brother could not find work, times were indeed hard and people were very bitter and unhappy. But in spite of all this terrible situation, one did not get the violence and wicked acts, we do get in this age. I do wonder, does todays behaviour stem from the aftermath of two wicked Wars. The values of today are nil compared to my early years, and I think all those left, of my generation must think the same way.

Well my life was set to change as we go into nineteen twenty and I can still live a lot of the agony although it is so long ago. My dear old Gran still lived with us and like I said before, even her meagre pension did help, we had a very, very low income, as did every one who lived close by, I could tell you many heart ache stories about peoples lives, but don't want you too dismayed, only thankful that your lot is much better and will always stay that way. Well what happened, now the Flu outbreak was still lingering on, and didn't pass our door, but came in and created loss undreamt of by any one of us. My Gran was the first victim, but by the "Grace of God" pulled through as did myself.

Then my dad caught it and was very ill, and I don't want to think that medical help might have saved him had it been more caring but I know in my heart that was so. This was in the year nineteen twenty, and April, my mom was thirty six on the second of this month. She gave birth to her eighth baby on the twenty fourth, I told you we only had two bedrooms and a large attic, the children shared, myself included. We had two good sized beds but not a surplus of bedding, and we were very decent and shared. My Gran had the small back room, my Mom, dad the front bedroom. I am telling you all this so you can compare Brum and it's way of life then and now.

I also told you all people's lanes had tears and laughter, this part of mine was flooded with tears, and I couldn't sweep them away, they were lasting so long and not a break in the clouds. During the night on the twenty third my Gran called me from sleep to go and get the midwife who lived ten min's away, no handy phones in those days, my dads job, but far too ill by now. I ran for a very kind aunty who lived close at hand, but first stoking up the fire to get hot water, still no gas stove. She lived in Floodgate Street and was a homely sort of person who had delivered all my brothers and sisters. I think my aunt and I ran all the way to get her , and that black bag. This baby arrived and was a lovely bonny little girl, with my mom's lack of the worlds goods, I can't understand how, "Gods Will" I reckon. I remember carrying her in to the back room to show my dad, who barely looked at her, he was far too ill, and so my little sister never had a daddy. My dad had two sisters who lived in Bearwood, a very pretty area at this time, they were comfortably off and proved to be angels to me when I certainly needed them. I think they took Gran, their mother, to one of their homes, she was only just recovering from the flu, and gone a little deaf, which really annoyed her.

I was kept very busy now, looking after my other brothers and sisters, tending fires upstairs and down. The neighbours could not have done more than they did, bringing me coal, and dainty bits for my mom & dad, it was not easy to give away in those days, they all owned so little, but what a different spirit existed then as today, which is why I am telling you about this part of my lane. The part of our journey, we now take, I call my valley of tears because I certainly shed a lot. I heard "David Jacobs" speak about his loss a little while back, how true what he said. Years and Years roll away but a thought can trigger off a memory and the tears and pain comes back, but not quite so intense.

Well to get back to my Mom, Dad, and this part of this my memory lane, I do not find it easy to tell you about this length of my lane, but I must tell you all or nothing. My Mom got me to help her to see my dad in that other small room, the last time she saw him. He died on the 27th April, it was Tuesday lunch time and I was with him. I railed at such a cruel fate, he was such a very good husband and father, and to me a wonderful Pal who as never been replaced. I told my mom and she never shed one tear, but said you were the best husband in the world Alf, and I will soon be with you. I now had another problem, my little sister who was eighteen months old and my young brother who was four years old, went down with the deadly flu. I got on the tram to take my little sister to Dr. Wilkinson by Bordesley station, she was a bit much to carry for me . The doctor was kind but found it hard to accept my dad was dead and my mom not able to take her to see him. He told me to go home and he would visit, which he did, he got an ambulance and my little brother and sister went to Erdington infirmary, both of them very ill.

I stayed with my Mom by day and night, popping in to keep looking at my darling dad all the time. In those days, were kept in their coffins and not taken away like today. The new baby was lovely but I needed my good neighbour and Gods help to help me take care of her. This part of my story, will help you understand how 70 yrs as brought such wonderful changes to all our lives and may it continue to do so. I made my Mom a cup of tea and she still couldn't cry, although I begged her to, and said to me out of the blue, our little Elsie is flying around this room. That made me cry and worry because this was my little sister in hospital who was on a special pass as was my brother. This is another thing to note compared to today's visit to hospitals. No one was allowed passed the hospital entrance without a pass, they were issued to close relatives only, and for certain days and times unless on a Special. I went as often as I could, and my life long friend Ada went with me each time. They were in the same ward on opposite sides of the room and we changed places to sit by each bed in turn.

It's wonderful how the new baby survived through all this turmoil and sorrow. My dad was to be buried on the following Tuesday and on the Monday I went to get my Black from Moor St. Warehouse. I kissed my Mom and baby sister, and said I would be as quick as possible. I think that day gave me the biggest shock of my young life, and I have had quite a few knocks. When I entered our street from Deritend I knew something was wrong by the people gathered in groups by our house. My kind neighbour who was going in to tend my Mom, held me close and could hardly give me the terrible news. My Mom had died in her sleep and her baby was nestled in her arms. Then once more Dr. Wilkinson came in when called and he was a perfect gentleman, I believe he was on the bench at the "Law Courts". He was very kind, and also upset at this turn of events, and he told me my Mom died of a broken heart, but could not put this on the report. So now I had two coffins in this house, which I hated for ever after, and I was frightened for the future of us all. But I had too much to do to let my grief take over, but I never dreamt there was more to come.

The undertaker "Mr. Wheatley" arranged everything for us even to keeping the grave open at Witton, and my Mom being a Catholic it was more trouble for him, and I do remember his goodness more so because we had such little

40

Flu that left us orphans

Another Birmingham widow has recalled the help she and her family received from The Birmingham Mail Christmas Tree Fund in the 1920s.

Mrs. M. Houghton of Yardley Wood has enclosed what she calls her "widow's mite", a £1 donation towards the £40,000 appeal.

Mrs. Houghton was prompted to write when she read a letter from Edith Hughes, who is now in New Zealand.

Dinner

"I went to the same school as Edith," she writes.

"I remember your wonderful Fund, without which in 1920, my brothers and sisters and myself would have been without a Christmas Dinner.

"My parents had just died, leaving me at 16 years old with seven children to care for, no Social Services, but just the Board of Guardians — a fine body with no soul.

Sight

"That terrible outbreak of flu after the first world war robbed me of both my parents in one week — and they were only 37-years old.

"I never did know who pushed the Fund ticket under our door. I had to go to the barracks in Thorp Street. I was not very big and struggled back home with one or maybe two large carriers.

The goods were arranged all around the yard in the barracks on trestles.

"What a wonderful sight!

"A grand piece of beef, tea, sugar, everything to make Christmas Day a joy — or nearly so.

"So please God you can go on helping, because in this land of plenty there is always someone very grateful to receive".

Mrs. Houghton is right.

Thousands of applications from the old and needy are now being considered.

£40,000

Nan remembers with thanks the assistance she received over 60 years before

55

so called (Good Old Days) It seemed my Mom & Dad' called her to rest with them, one of their brood, which left seven of us. Well I think we could rest awhile now, whoever of my family are walking my lane with me. We have travelled 16 yrs and a half, so far, but you did ask and I warned you, its was rather long. I have now changed from a girl who had known only love even in deep poverty, to a frightened young woman. What was I going to do? without my caring parents, who had carried all our lives carting along. We had no "Social Services" never even dreamt of in those far off days, we did have a "Board of Guardians", who you steered clear of for as long as possible. I had six brothers and sisters, the darling beautiful baby of ten days old, and now a real good mother herself, and one of my loved one's still. I look back and know that at this time 'God' was with me all the way and surrounded me with neighbours that dont come any more, not needed so badly any more, because of a better standard

Page 55 of Nan's Original Narrative

money to pay him. I have said before about big hearted Brummies and no more proof was needed at this time in my life. Collections went on in every quarter of Deritend, streets and factories alike. My Uncle from Bearwood opened a joint post office account and I'll talk about it later. It is very hard to explain the difference of a funeral today and then. Everything was Black, known as deep mourning, and lasted for a year, then changed to half mourning purple or mauve or grey. The Hearse was carried along very very slowly by beautiful Black horses, what an awful drawn out agony that was. I won't enlarge on this, we got to Witton and we came back.

I can hardly collect my thoughts about all this, it's all so very unreal and cruel. In those far off days death was very morbid and made worse by everything around it. My Mom was laid to rest on the Saturday morning and no light let in until the Sunday next day. But in my case not even then, I had opened up three out of four windows and my dear neighbour called to me upstairs to close them again. We had an inmate from the infirmary, with a note to say my darling little Elsie had passed away, that's how you were informed in those so called "good old days". It seemed my Mom & dad called her to rest with them, one of their brood, which left seven of us. Well I think we could rest awhile now, whoever of my family are walking my lane with me.

We have travelled 16 yrs. and a half so far, but you did ask and I warned you, it was rather long. I have now changed from a girl who had known only love, even in deep poverty, to a frightened young woman. What was I going to do? without my caring parents, who had carried all our lives calmly along. We had no "Social Services" never even dreamt of in those far off days, we did have a "Board of Guardians", who you steered clear of for as long as possible. I had six brothers and sisters, the darling beautiful baby of ten days old, and now a real good mother herself, and one of my loved ones still.

I look back and know that at this time "God" was with me all the way and surrounded me with neighbours that don't come any more, not needed so badly any more, because of a better standard of living. We have all got emotions, and I knew only one until now at this time, it had been pure family love, but now it was lost to one stronger than all, and even now without that wonderful help from above, Fear can take over our lives. This is were I ask you all my children, grand and great, to fight this terror and seek the help I have got all my life and I am not deeply religious, but I do truly believe.

But now back to the task in hand, and what was I going to do.? My Gran was still with us, and that gave the home a figure head, and God Bless her memory, she was wonderful. She had just lost her youngest son , my dad, but her faith was always quiet and very strong. I had still got a job in the foundry were my dad had worked, but two or three days a week only if I was lucky, work was terribly short, and could not get better. My Mom's good neighbour had the baby most of the day time, and I took over at night. My biggest worry now was finding the right kind of food for this new baby, I went to the "Welfare" as we called it, got her weighed, had a visitor call to see how we were coping and that was that. I now find it so hard to believe that all this happened, but is 70 yrs ago, and just a way of life of those poor far off days. I tried all kinds of food for my little baby and somehow, something must have suited, because she is still with us (Thank God). I could name a lot of these things, we still have them on the shop shelves (Sorry Teacher).

My little brother is very very ill and I am at my wits end with worry over him. Dear God don't take him from me I pray, I'm losing all I love. He was spared but did not come home, after a while he went into the "Cottage Homes" at "Marston Green" and stayed there for roughly twelve years. This was a very hard time for me, I could not have him home, he was far from well or strong. These homes were comprised of cottages, so many children in each, and all had a Mother. The visiting was very poor and one had to watch "Saturday" evening Mail for instructions maybe three or four months between each visit, and I can't remember losing one in all those years. My brother grew up knowing only me, not as his sister but "Miss" who always came to see him, and he always asked me if I would take him home with me.

I still look back, as now, and wonder were did I get all my tears from, I sure had a good supply at this time of my life. This phase of my life had to pass as they all did, but you will note then and now, Marston Green was reached by train from New St. Station. A very small place, dark, lit by lamp, and terribly cold all those winters ago, but who cared about conditions, we Mothers and families, got a little stay with those we dearly loved, and could not for different reasons cuddle at home. We could buy a cup of tea in the old 'Lea Hall' tavern while waiting for the train home, and another memory was imprinted in my longish lane. I am now wondering what was going to happen next, it could not get harder but ease up a little, usually did.

Well back to my family, eh kids, are you still with me, or had enough. I'm going to finish, I started because you all asked. I now have one beautiful baby and she certainly was that, and her life had got to take shape, and I had to help in this case one way or another. The next youngest now is my brother Charlie who was seven years old and believe me "all boy" as he still is, although an Old one now. Then I have a pretty "Green eyed" sister Emmie who at this time was ten years old, and my next oldest sister who was, and still is one of the finest gentle little girls of all time. My brother Bill whom I lost four years ago, was now struggling what to do for the best, no work, no future, doing his best to help, but so little he could do, and he had been the apple of my Mom's eye which was quite right he was her first son. My Gran was still our guardian angel, old, but quite capable and still meant we could keep together so far. We

44

had rumblings of Dr. Barnardo's home and how nice it was in Canada, but my Uncle Jim would have none of it and took charge in a bigger way. I find some of this a bit hazy at times, am I having a real bad dream, and the house will be back to normal. Now a thing happened that could not by any means happen today. Something was said at a Mass in St. Ann's Catholic Church up the street in Alcester St., a baby was in need of adoption, just like that it seems, a couple of people came to look at my baby and what they saw they liked. They were not young, but also not old, and very good folks. My sister went with them, nothing legal about it, no name change, and the baby started her new life.

It is so hard to believe all this could have happened, but it did, and as always will be "truth" is stranger than fiction. We still have a few pounds in our joint account and dished out by my Uncle each Sat. morning when I met him outside his factory in "Summer Lane" were he worked as a foreman, good job at that time, but he was a good living caring man, and was the means of us staying together as we did. But this bit of income could not go on for ever, and it was the money gathered by the neighbours that had been quite good, but I never knew how much and it didn't seem to matter really, it had been a "God Send". My brother bless him joined the army and made a grand soldier just as his dad had. He did 21 yrs. but broke his service and got no pension. He was in the occupation army in Germany but also went to other places and did not feel he was a worry to me any more. He made me an allowance of seven shillings a week, and I tried hard not use it, so he had a little when he got home on leave.

I am now really worried about what's happening in my lane, how things change in a short time, and we have to stand still, and watch it all take place. I can't remember exact dates but my sister Emmie was just of ten yrs. old and I lost another of my family which I really did because we lost all track of each other. My Uncle learned of people with a flourishing shop, I won't give names or places in this case , it would not be fair to my sister or her new parents. My uncle and I took my two sisters Annie & Emmie to this shop and though they had wanted one a little younger, they decided to take Emmie. Poor Annie, they had a piano and a very nice home. This was all done by proper channels, Legal adoption and name change.

I have a smaller family now, haven't I? but we are still poor like everyone around us, but when we have a big worry, didn't use that word problem so much, it was a worry so we always got to work on it, we pulled and dragged at it until it vanished and made room for the next, which always did come, no doubt about that at all. I don't know how long before things got a bit more settled but we still had to find the rent and firing, not much looking back, but it was an awful lot to us. I had an old, very old sewing machine my dad had bought me to learn on, I think he was ambitious for his eldest daughter and maybe she would become a dressmaker, a good standing all those years ago, you didn't buy from the peg those days. I sold this old contraption for four pounds, a good price really, must have had a sympathetic buyer, can't think of any other reason. I don't recall too much about it really, only that I did get "Charlie Boy" some new boots and a couple of little shirts, so that was not too bad, at all.

Well we are still using lamps and candles, but quite a few houses around now had gas and cookers at this time. But I think we got more memory pictures by my poor old lighting, than from fast becoming gas. I think you may sum up this one with me and maybe a little smile, my Gran is sitting in her old rocking chair, specs' on her nose and very serious in the job at hand. She is sewing on a large white patch on a sheet, toe nails she blamed for all these holes, not old age sheets. This is were I have a good word for candle light or lamp, it did not seem to matter, was the patch straight, round or what, as long as she covered that blooming hole. This light did no harm to all shape stitches, as long as that patch got on the sheet which did get washed and hung outside, back of the house and on the line. We had no washing machines, blow driers, only old mangles which were a God send to our Moms with such large broods to keep clean.

I think we can leave this house now, and get into our lane once more, a long way to go yet kids. Around this time I suppose it was I got a surprise, I heard a small commotion outside in the street, all our doors led directly on to the street. I stood on the steps and froze I think. A lovely side car was looking at me, and I saw my "Emmie" sitting in it, I don't recall much or anything, only my sister there dressed so prettily, who had been brought to show me how well she was being cared for. The last time I saw her dressed in smart leopard skin coat and hat, and then "Good bye". This was just one more barb in my poor old heart, and it still hurts funnily enough.

We will leave "Charlie Boy" and Annie, my Mom's name if I haven't mentioned it already, playing Ludo, Snakes and ladders or reading, and no doubt a little puzzled by all that was taking place around them. We have to come back to this house some time for the rest of this Saga. We still have town criers I know, but they were more than plentiful in those streets of Brum so long ago, and most were called "Mom", now and again it could have been dad. If we pass an open door out come the sounds, no secrets here. Mom he's got my shoe lace, . . . He won't give me the towel, . . . I'll be late for school, . . . can't find the button hook, . . . Use an hair pin then, . . . Oh my God, give me that cane, I'll use it this time by God I will.

I'll leave you with the sound of the "Brummie" Town Cry's, and if you are still with me, this time should have been half way (maybe) of the nineteen twenties. I can't be sure of holding your interest now, because I'm in a crowd of Brummies of so long ago but all so very clear to me. Each face, every voice and I am touching them all in my mind. I see my Ada's face laughing in

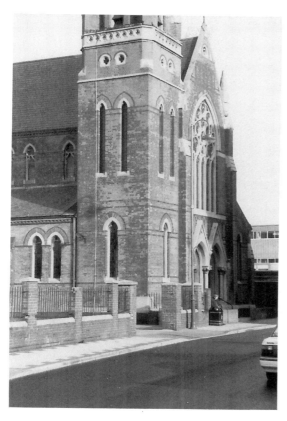

St. Anne's Roman Catholic Church
Deritend

Peggy
Lizzie's youngest sister
who was in her mothers arms
at the time of death

Plaque on site of St. John's Church
Deritend

The Spotted Dog – Alcester Street

the centre of them, and will tell you now this was and still is all about real Friends, who never die. She is resting in Yardley Cemetery with her beloved hubby Tom, in a grave. I won't harp on this part, but neither will it pass unnoticed. You, my older kids knew her as "Aunty Ada", and maybe this will help you learn what real Friendship stands for, I hope without preaching, a lot of my history will do just that. If you want to move along while I ponder, it's not too far to go along Alcester St. to dear old Highgate park alongside "Rowton House" the home of so many human working machines.

The "Navvy", he loved to get drunk at the weekend, fall down, challenge the "Coppers", so called then, finish up in Moseley St. Police station right close at hand. I think this part of my past is more funny than harmful (my opinion) perhaps and we can take note of a Drunk then and now. He usually done himself the most harm (not always I know) he was fined on Monday morning, at the court in Corporation St, touched his cap to the bench, worked hard digging the roads all the week, hoping to repeat his performance at the next weekend. We were not inflicted with real violence then "Thank God" we had enough to contend with. The police today are having a wicked time, then we called them our friends very much respected, and they stood for "Law and Order", I don't see much of this around today, just plenty of it talked about.

I'll get back into lane a little way along Alcester St, I think I have already mentioned this part of my life, because this was my love, my candle and lamplight part for so many years. This is not easy writing now really, I want to hold your interest whichever one of you is trudging my "Memory Lane". But after all they are my people and I can't expect you to see all these faces in front of me. I could fit a real tale to each one because they are not "Fiction" and made "Brum" in it's Birthday year, and I still see it as the "Best Place" in the World. I can say it and mean it, because, of these later years I have done many visits to places I never dreamt in my wildest dreams of seeing. I take it you have had enough, and walked to my dear old park, I'll tell you why I call it this later.

We had a wonderful Old Church, just around in Deritend, St. John's by name, I can't with truth say how old it was, but I always saw it in my mind in all those fields on the River Rea. This is were "Our Nan" can meditate, shall I go into Church were I married and you my three wonderful girls were Christened. But I can also be happy, not a loosely termed expression, by popping into the "Spotted Dog" for half a pint of real Cold Ale, still there but with many alterations I reckon, and it could choke me with memory. A terrible thing did happen at this point I can't let pass, it brought to light the age of Deritend for us. A group of youngsters two of mine among them were playing in a big yard adjoining the pub. A little boy vanished down a hole in the ground, it was a wicked gas filled Well, the top had caved in, swallowed the dear little soul. I think it took two days and nights to recover the body. I don't suppose his life could have been saved even today, but it would have been quicker. We did not have, seventy years ago the machinery of today, another thing to be thankful for now. The sad part of this story, little Lesley was being looked after by his Aunt and Uncle, who lived in this yard by the pub. His Mom was dying in hospital and so wasn't told if I recall rightly.

Well I can't stay with my group of Brummies for ever but I will say after all these years, I can put a name and face to every one of them, that's because they were and still are real people. Well now I'm getting confused I was going to take you along to my Park along Alcester St, and don't know if I have already mentioned it. But I have just been reading "Fred Norris'" in our "Evening Mail" and he made me laugh, papers don't seem to do much of that these days do they? It seems he had found "Brummie" language all around the World. So the mention of Park as given me the most sweet tender memory of them all. I want you to picture Our Nan, that's me as a little girl about ten or eleven maybe years old. We get a lot of contrasts with today in this one.

It seems you stop being a little girl now at about six yrs old and know as much as I did at nine or ten. This certainly don't seem possible, but believe me, when I can hardly believe myself, what over seventy years as done to us all. Well here we go, Mom is standing on our step, and I am being given my orders, they were given and taken, no asking what it's worth, like today. I am in charge of the "Babby", we only said Baby if we lived in a Rd. not a street (joke). I don't know now if it's a boy or girl, but we always had one in our house like all the other folks around us. This one is seated in an old wooden push chair, strapped safely in, laughing and eager to be away. I've got an handy carrier, no plastic bags then, and Mom as made the bottom safe with padded newspaper. She tells me to mind how I cross the road, only one with tram lines to cross. We always get a pair of hands to say thank you to, for helping us to cross, so Mom does not have to worry. She gets on with the housework and meal getting, for when dad gets home, God Bless him. So off with the push chair we go. I remember it well, this one had a mind of it's own, but the wheels played a big part in the journey. The side streets always beckoned my transport instead of straight ahead. I am getting nearer Highgate Park now, and so is one other big sister, but this is a bigger pram, and carries two passengers and a bigger handy carrier nestled between them.

We are not in a race. Oh no I see it as a mission, (not impossible), "Our Nan" will do it, you'll see. I have reached the gate, now the fun starts, it's open planning now, but not then. You have to slide in, work around, but for some reason you always get trapped. The Park Keeper as is eye on you, always as, but no help expected and you get none. So out comes the little un, prop him or her up against the rails, with the handy carrier, fold the chair up, and struggle inside park. I take a quick look along the street, the other pram is going to turn into "Darwin St". It as to pass a few very nice houses, and just a few shops, I could name them all, and what they sold but they have all completely gone, only still worth holding in my memory a bit of my dear 'Old Brum'. The girl with the pram can enter through a side street, and it will bring her further into the park, I can't let her have my favourite seat, were I mean to sit and watch boys and men at play. I know nothing of, bowls, cricket or the like but I enjoy watching. I liken some of these people to those on the pictures, a few good silent ones around at this time. We did Sat. morning matinees and think it was a penny to go. This may not interest you at all, but how simple was life then, set by today's standards.

I know how long I can stay but wonder, because I had no watch, but could always ask the time. We had no fears at this time at asking strangers anything, but always use our manners. I am going back through the straight gate, the way of the pram longer, but much easier on me and the bab. Maybe this is not much to dwell upon, but I feel good, don't know anything at this time about being happy or sad. We all seemed to take what ever came along. Reached home safely, Mom & dad pleased with me, my reward more than enough.

You ask, why my best tender memory? looking back now on my eighty sixth birthday, I see many reasons. At this stage I am around ten years old, I can hardly compare this with the same age today. We can't fairly compare anything, then and now, such a different environment, same World. Well you asked for memories, I just thought of Brum candles, lamps, and faces of so many bygone friends. But I have not lost them all, Oh No, I have cards staring at me now from Australia, America, one in mind only, from New Zealand, and nearer home Cornwall and all around this area, even from the Black Country, many of these my Children, Grand, and now 'how lovely' Great, so I am indeed 'One Lucky Lady', not forgetting nieces, my "Bill's" family. This is were I once again say "Thank God".

Well I must get this lot a bit ship shape not easy you must agree, I'm all over the place, and our Gran has still got an eye on Charlie Boy and Annie. But I did keep her until she was ninety six, and it set another poser, which I can't answer, don't know if you can. How come, looking at my age group and there are a lot of us, survived such a lot of worries, heart aches and lack-ofs. Maybe perhaps with our backs always to the wall, we saw our enemy, biggest one 'Poverty', and we had a jolly good fight. I reckon it was better than all those staged today, with a big Money Carrot dangling on the ropes, we enjoyed eating our carrots, part of our 'Menu'. I am now going to close my lane, and enter streets, but remember you can all have a lovely gently winding lane for you and your loved one's, keep it as "God " intended, full of his "wonderful handy" work, and not choked like our streets, with "Man Made possessions".

51

How do we all get involved from now on, I'm just hoping you are not all sorry you started this. I love it, and my good doctor knows it's better for me than his pills, but they have done me good (don't tell him). I think these streets could now be in the nineteen thirties, please don't study dates too much, I can only cope with events happening around this time, and plenty was, believe me. The scars of War were with us, not in broken buildings, that came later didn't it? but full of broken promises, despair and feeling hopeless. But once again help, again from dear "Old Brummies", and I am going to name these from my past, as this kind of work they did should never ever be forgotten, and not based on my opinions, but real stark fact. You all and me, have got many benefits from the 'missions' they set themselves to achieve. Dear little "Percy Shurmer", full of fire and brimstone, having a go at anything, that he could see was hurting his "Brummie Clan". He gathered a good crowd of followers. Freddie Longton the boy, who refused to go to War and went to Prison instead. We were supposed to be fighting for freedom, where were his rights, do we still only have these rights when it suits the book. I am going to set many posers now, and you can find the answers, have a go kids. I've tried too long and I can sit and watch you all, but I must pray hard, because I really think they are more deadly than those we had. I am not very old at this point, but maybe the way we dressed at this time didn't help, and yet again strangely enough I see fashions today looking much like those in the "Old Weldon's" book of fashion, still on the peg. I married in nineteen twenty six, and apart from you my three wonderful daughters it doesn't seem to matter much about this part.

Well before I leave Percy and his wonderful gang, "Batman and Robin" are poor shadows of what they were or did. I should imagine this was about the time "Unions and Labour Party" came into our lives, some one had to do something, and as now, someone will always come along, and we the people hope it's for the good. I look back and think this was not too bad a time, not good by any means, but what is a good time to live in ?. Charles Dickens, William Shakespeare, went with me to school in Floodgate St, and I don't recall their lives being easy, so I think a lot is in a "State of Mind", and we all have some control over that.

Work was creeping in slowly, and wages certainly so, but money had been found for War and this fact keeps the "Rebel" in your Nan very much alive. Why did not my "Mom and Dad" have a bit more of it?, it must have been there, it was used to make munitions, invent tanks and to kill and destroy. But all this is so long ago, only I do know that a lot of today stems from yesterday. I suppose we have caught up a lot with our "Man Power" loss, and boys without dads are growing into another generation another World almost, to mine, but this will always have to be so. If I stay in this street a little longer, it's still there but only the "Spotted Dog" on the corner of 'Warwick St.' to

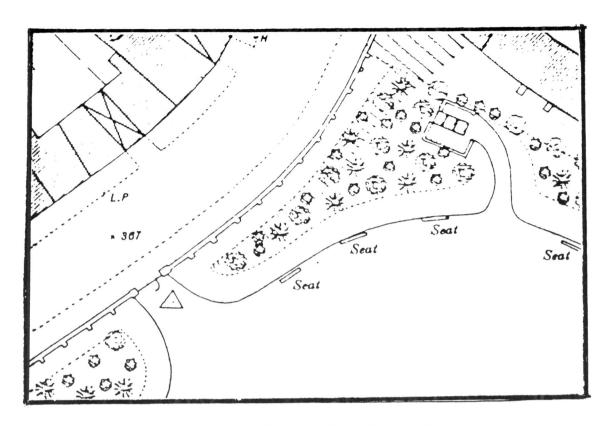

Highgate Park: Entrance from Alcester Street
that 'Babbies Gate' in Lizzie's day

The entrance from Alcester Street, 1995

Lizzie and colleagues working at Fisher's Foundry, Albion Road, Greet, 1940
Left to right: Back Row
– Freda – Mary – May – Ted – Violet
Front row
– ? – Auntie Lizzie – Lizzie (Nan) – Alice –
Who is the lady in the dark overall?

A friend from the foundry

WAY back in early 1940 I went to work in a foundry with many other young women. We were a jolly set of pals, but for me one became special.

I badly needed a friend at that time for many private reasons. I had three young daughters and my friend became an auntie to them. Now, after all these years, she is still that auntie and my special friend.

We went through air raids, shortages, good and bad times and laughter and tears. I doubt if many of our old pals are left. Although we are now widows we are still going strong and sharing all that comes along.

I am treating these last few years as a bounty and thanking God for my wartime pal from the Black Country.

From MRS. HOUGHTON, Birmingham.

Mrs Houghton (nee Shott)

54

recreate a picture for me. We were getting a bit more pleasure from life, "Ada" staunch firm laughing friend as she always was. The Picture houses were coming into their own, but taking over our "Music Halls". I can't begin to name those wonderful artistes of that time, spreading love and laughter in every town were they played, talent so plentiful one wonders were it came from, money never came. they had enough for humble homely digs, and a tram ride or train, one for the next booking.

We saw "Gracie Fields" our very own, with "Archie Pitts" in "Mr Tower of London" at our "Old Empire" which we may have called the "Tivoli" in those days. We had wonderful Rep', at the Alex' and our Show palaces, like Theatre Royal and Prince of Wales gave us names that will never be forgotten. But close at hand, just in Bordesley, we had our own personal Palace owned by Mrs Kimberly and her daughter Ruby, you will never hear sounds like those again, that came floating into the streets outside. We had laughter, smiles and even mild swearing, if the villain had gone over the top. Across the road in Bordesley were a couple of pubs and, those who cared to could have a pass out, and run across for a pint, the show was never ruined because the pubs had a bell to warn the show was coming back on stage. I tell you this my darlings because at this time, this was still my "Brum" and part of every day life.

I ask myself now, was this a quality of life, of course it's gone for ever, but how can we improve on all the simple things that gave it to us, I do know this answer, it's a big No, its yesterday and gone for ever. I don't want to bore you, but my tears are still shed for this period of my becoming a woman. I reckon our homes showed a bit more signs of wealth, we could get furniture on hire, yours when you finished paying. Bentley, was a good firm down Deritend selling real wood and leather goods, I still own a few remnants.

We had a very obliging Provident agent, a cheque would help you and the kids, to look different on "Sunday", just clean and tidy all the week. But wait for this gem, I laugh now at the sight, but it is also a memory I can touch and still see. Our Provident man, I could, but won't name him, can't be sure he would have wanted me to. Well he came around for orders for pianos, I don't know if any one said No to this one, I didn't, my girls were to have lessons, only they never did, sooner play rounders with the boys up the back yards. Mine is still with us, and in my eldest girls home absolutely lovely and after 50 yrs. it's not anything like "Old Fashioned". But not too long after delivery came orders for returns, after all they did cost thirty pounds or maybe a little over, and three shill's a week was a bit much, and a couple of bob for the clothes cheque. But believe me girls, it was great fun watching the firm trying to get them back. All these doors we were supposed never to lock, took on the role of "Fort Knox".

But like I say this was "Brum" coming out of the Doldrums, and we meant to do it with music. I know all I am saying can be proved, if you went were a lot of Men and Ladies were now residing in homes provided, as against the Workhouse of long ago. They sing all these old songs with Glee, because like me, they stir up the memories and lovely "Old Lanes". Before Ada and myself settle down with marriage ties we did enjoy life, couldn't get my Mom & dad back could I? and they loved Ada for what she was, a kind unselfish friend and one to be trusted, but believe me when I say that we did have quite a few of those around then.

This gives you another Poser, (fed up are you with trying to get the answers?) I'm still at it also. Why is everything today tarnished with Gold, Jewels, Cars and the biggest Mansion money can buy. We managed without, just content when we got our own bathrooms instead of running across the yard to the wash house. I am asking silly questions, because it will still be going on when you are all Great or more, parents, and maybe on the moon at that.

To come back a bit and our pleasures, we loved all the boy's sports, I suppose because they did not need a lot of money, only a puncture outfit for our dear old bikes. We used to go and watch the "Blues" play, one shilling on "Spion Cop" and one & six behind the goal posts. Oh my poor voice, and perhaps I can stick with this one for a while, because the contrasts are so great, and very hard to believe. I am sorry I am meandering a bit, quite a bit, because it really is about Brum " Then and Now". We shall get back to my Gran, but I did keep her until she was ninety six, so I will now ask you to be with me around nineteen twenty four and six. Real dates don't really matter, we are dealing with true facts and my opinion, and my dear "Old Brum".

I expect you to differ with me a lot of the time, as to how I weighed things up, but that could keep you a bit interested. I only wanted to talk, or write rather about my "Memories" and lamp and candle light, and you are getting about eighty years of it, but then this is what you wanted, I hope. The whole country is in on this one, not just "Brum" or local towns and I may be involving and not one of you see any sense in it, but here goes.

I'm right inside this crowd with Ada and our "Boy Friends". I want you to form in your mind, two pictures, one, Black and or mostly Grey, 'then' ; now another one, in Colour, this one being, 'now'. I'm dealing with the 'then' crowd understand, and we are in the centre of it. It is a Sat. afternoon, the weather could be anyhow, but sure to be cold at this time of year, football season. I've told you about prices and I've told you before, what a lot we got for a shilling. Down our street came a crowd, you will never ever see again, poorly clad, men, boys and a few ladies, we are all absolutely "Blues City Mad", all laughing, joking and the banter wonderful. If there was swearing we never heard it, and of course there must have been some, I'm not so silly to think otherwise. A big lesson I think here, self respect and discipline, just caring about the other one in this crowd, can you find any of it today?. Maybe you know the answer, I don't. I suppose a policeman was here and there, but

That 'Fort Knox' Piano
and
the Paid up Receipt

PROVIDERS OF
RATIONAL CREDIT
FACILITIES to the
PIANO INDUSTRY
In Association with
Triumph Auto Pianos Ltd
Barratt & Robinson Ltd

TRIUMPH AUTO SALES LTD.
(1930)

288/310. YORK WAY. LONDON. N.7

TELEPHONE
NORTH 4021/2
(EXTENSION TO ALL DEPTS.)
TELEGRAMS :
KASTOREN
HOLWAY LONDON

DIRECTORS
G. L. WATES. F. H. SAFFELL. R. W. KING. R. MONTGOMERIE

| March, 1937. | To "Saffell" Piano in Mahogany No. 19148. | £39. 18. 0 |
| | | Nett. |

2039

16th Apl 1946   £   s.   d.
Received from   39 = 18 = 0
Mrs M Houghton
Birmingham
FOR
TRIUMPH AUTO SALES
1930 LTD.
Thirty Nine Pds Eighteen Shlgs

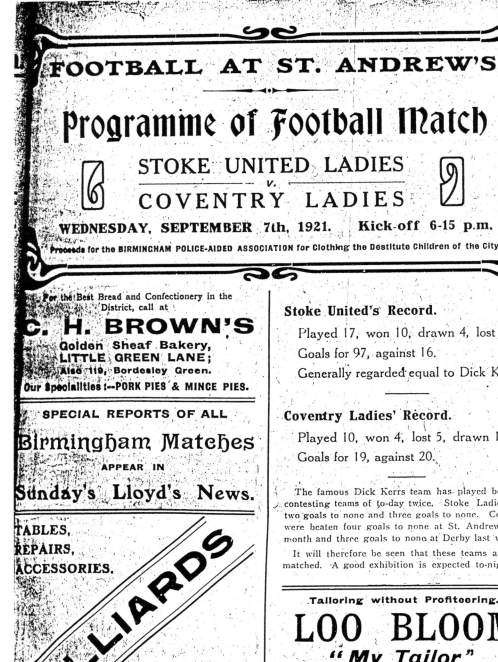

FOOTBALL AT ST. ANDREW'S.

Programme of Football Match

STOKE UNITED LADIES
v.
COVENTRY LADIES

WEDNESDAY, SEPTEMBER 7th, 1921. | **Kick-off 6-15 p.m.**

Proceeds for the BIRMINGHAM POLICE-AIDED ASSOCIATION for Clothing the Destitute Children of the City.

Stoke United's Record.

Played 17, won 10, drawn 4, lost 3.

Goals for 97, against 16.

Generally regarded equal to Dick Kerrs.

Coventry Ladies' Record.

Played 10, won 4, lost 5, drawn 1.

Goals for 19, against 20.

The famous Dick Kerrs team has played both the contesting teams of to-day twice. Stoke Ladies lost two goals to none and three goals to none. Coventry were beaten four goals to none at St. Andrew's last month and three goals to none at Derby last week.

It will therefore be seen that these teams are well matched. A good exhibition is expected to-night.

. . . a mid-week match, smashing . . .
and advertisements of the day

mostly to hold up the traffic, trams and horses as we crossed Deritend, Bordesley or Digbeth. I told you it was a big crowd, and no doubts you could get figures even now at "Blues City Offices".

Ada and I far from being tall, so we had to move sharply along to get a chance of a good view, no worry here, we always did thanks to the poorly clads of so long ago. This is a long, long time ago my darlings and I still can see the players in long shorts and real boots, we knew them all by name because they were footballers not men who had been sold like animals. We sometimes had a bad game, who doesn't at any sport? but what happened after this match? I think I saw tears at times, I'll say that anyhow. We have lost and got to go out on the streets, and it's always colder than when you win. In front of every house all around " Small Heath" and up every back yard, are poor boys minding, not stealing bikes, for those spectators who came a longer journey, and you had better believe me they did. It always took longer to walk home when you lost, but not to worry no one was going to get hurt, no people, no police and no broken windows.

We did have a mid-week match once, smashing, that was "Dick Kerrs" eleven and nearly certain they played Stoke ladies. These were "Ladies" can you even think of such an event taking place today? The dads went home and Moms were always on his side what ever he said about the team. If they could afford a pint and not too heart-broken, an hour in the local, on that cold Grey night might just put that team right. Well I can see many lessons in this little picture, maybe some of you can but that will not alter one little thing that is happening right now, even while I'm scribbling, I have two words and one is so important, but it's 'winning' all along the line.

We can now put on the other picture, and it's ugly, what my, then, picture never was in spite of it's poverty. I am not trying to find a cure, a lot of money is being spent now in that direction, and I can't see it doing any good in my life time, may be in some of yours, which I very much doubt, because the game is dying. I can't walk with this now crowd, because, the first reason, hardly any do walk, they come in cars. First Problem here, word I hate, but the only one to explain, is the mind on the game? or were they can park, no matter were it may be, and their worry in case it's stolen, or smashed. Next query, can they get a couple of pints before they enter the grounds, I am referring to any football ground now, not just my "Blues", all around the country if not the world

It is years since I went to a match but we can watch T.V. and it's rarely one can get real joy. Who's that player? ...Oh, they just bought him from so-and-so, he cost nearly a quarter of a million... Does one man make a team now? It wasn't that way in my Then Games was it? This should have made a pretty coloured picture, all the trapping here, "No one cold" whatever the Sat. afternoon weather. Flasks on the hips, not all I know, but I'm angry when I look back and see what as happened to that game, so beloved of long ago, by the men who had so little of any of this worlds goods, but still knew how to behave like real men. They, had memories of boys dying in trenches, who never got a chance to see a game, any kind of game.

My God, what a contrast, I don't have to dwell on the emptying of the ground after these matches, win or lose, maybe not always but not far off. I never knew we had so many Police, Panda Cars, Black Maria's etc. We are asking was it a good game how can you tell? ... Oh, that's trouble over in that corner ... now they are having a go at the Ref'..., and we did, but we only shouted ..."How's that Man, Ref."..., we had no desire to kill the player, the Ref., or hit the man standing next to you, on the head. Perhaps it's one way to get rid of the empties. I think I had better come off football don't you, but I think we are all hoping for any sport to get back to what it was before Drugs, money and a false way of life became fashion.

I freely say sorry kids if you think I'm blaming youth of today for all our troubles, we have only to cry for help for any terrible crisis, and you are all ready, it's taken years to get this standard of living, I brought you through it with me. So I am not putting all the blame on money and riches, but on War and our Generation that lived through it. We will talk this out some time because it is a very deep subject and I may be on my own with my opinions, and I've made myself sad, so if you like, I'm going back to my "Dear Old Gran", Charlie Boy and Annie.

I think before we do go, I should say one or two things I may not get back to. I only wanted to talk about my memories by Candle light, but you have really got me going my darlings. I may have you looking at pictures in your mind, because this is the only way to get a clear vision of what I am trying to say. My memories seem to be treasures in a Bank and I can get them out when I feel like glancing at them, or I have an "Old Curiosity shop" and it's full of old time pictures of people and their ways of long long ago. Well I don't want you to get too fed up with my travels, as we have a few years to go. But I do wonder one thing in this lot, did I bring the "handy carrier" home? I do know it was not on "Highgate Park" ground, not with that Park Keeper, he had eyes every where. Oh Well.

When I get to Gran and the two young ones, I get a bit of trouble keeping it tidy. I've been standing still taking you back and moving forward, so you will have to help out and just dwell on events and near enough dates. I don't want to be too miserable so we will light the lamp, always a pleasure, my dads pride remember, build a nice glowing fire, and out with a few more memories. We do not have much more income, but I do a bit more work on and off, and I am working with my dad's "Old Mates". How cleverly they help you and you hardly see how a Moulder's wife suddenly finds a surplus of odds and ends, oh they might fit Charlie and Ann, they always did and at the time were a "God Send", which is what they were anyhow.

Our Gran only wanted a nice little spray of violets on her pretty Black satin bonnet, with it's wide silk ribbon to tie it. She always kept one of these hats in a round bonnet box, the one she wore all the time brushed and dusted kept handy, but did not have the same fuss spent on it. These sound such simple things which they were really, but they were to all a quality of life which took so little money to attain. Our Gran had never asked for much, but she enjoyed her half pint of ale and a crust of bread & cheese, every evening, this she had when "Mom and dad" were around, and this she had as long as I could manage it, and I always did, she deserved it.

I don't recall medals flying around at this time and the money that goes with them very often. There were only a few for the lads from the trenches and they ended up in pawn shops windows, (Nan is getting angry again). They are dished out today like you hand out lollipops to the children, to me they are worth nothing, and my Generation didn't need them, they had different ideas about duty. I must give a bit of time to my Charlie Boy and my dear gentle Annie. They are growing up and need decent clothing, these they did get and were an answer to a prayer, they were so grand and lovely at a time like this, only prayer could have taken care of it.

I have just realized we have not talked about one Xmas, and up to now we have had quite a few. Everyone tried to get a little something new at Christmas even in the poorest years. I can hear Church bells ringing on "Christmas Eve", people flocking to the Midnight Mass, what ever religion they were did not seem to matter so long as they remembered our "Lord's Birthday" and thank him for whatever they received in the coming Christmas week. The kiddies hung the black cashmere stockings on the end of the bed rails, and I dare say now, on looking back, it would have cost no more to fill half a dozen pairs, to what you pay for one Good pretty card now.

I am wandering all over this place now aren't I? but I am not writing a book, I am not clever enough for that, I respect anyone who can create characters and bring words from the mouths. I must rely on facts, thoughts and my own opinions, and you don't have to agree with all of them, dot them down on paper, and then say to each other 'Oh our Nan'. While I explain about Annie and Charlie's clothes, I get another picture, in nearly every house at this time you would see a pin cushion hanging by the fireplace, with plenty of pins sticking in it, and maybe a couple of needles. I think you may find the next bit hard to believe but anyone of my generation, and only as rich as I was, will tell you it was so. A neighbour would send one of the children to borrow a needle and cotton, black or white, to stitch something up before they could be off to school. In those good old days a reel of cotton would cost one halfpenny, but a reel of thread cost one penny, this really makes a contrast does it not? I'm going to call this a narrative and hope you don't all get fed up reading it, because we have a long way to go until we reach nineteen eighty nine.

I'll get back to children's clothes now and enjoy the thrill this gave me as well as my kids. We were getting a bit better off at this time all around us, but still hard pushed to buy really nice articles to wear, and these I did want for my Annie. Well this is how it all came about, me, I say it was an answered prayer, mine and our Gran's. The men at the foundry never stopped trying to help us even though Mom and Dad had left us a long time before. They got in touch with a Unionist man, that's what conservatives were called in those days, strange that. He was his own boss and came daily to the foundry in the cause of his job, he was waylayed about my position, and could he help in any way. He did just that, and as it was still the Board of Guardians, nothing was going to come easy.

I became the "Foster Mother" of Annie & Charlie, plenty of paper involved, here Gran was too old for this role, and I was a bit on the young side. But that's what I became and until this day that's how my Mom's family look on me, no other way really, I'm always in the picture. Well one day two new tin trunks arrived and we were afraid to open them, the children pictured Daily Mail clothes, good strong wearing stuff, but shouting out very loud of charity. We opened the lids, so the contents could be seen at the same time, and I know I must have shed a tear although I can't remember doing so now. Annie & Charlie each had three sets of clothing that's hard to describe, day and night, underwear, top wear, outdoor wear, boots, slippers, toilet bags containing tooth brushes etc. I could not retract all I had said about the "Board of Guardians" but I praised them then, and now, for the joy that came on those two faces, and Gran and myself "Thanked God".

This may seem a bit over the top now-a-days, because children all have some lovely clothes, ours do at least as you all provide. But if you followed me along my streets the story was so very different, and as a contrast, I can only say it was likened to winning the Pools now. I was also allowed a food amount for each one of them, I am not quite sure now how much that was, so long ago, but I think it was one pound fifteen shill's per week, plus they had milk, from our milkman, and the clothing allowance was very good, paid out every three months. I had a regular visitor, she was a wonderful understanding Lady, who never gave orders, because that was her job, but came at random to check I was doing my job properly as Foster Mother. We went to the shops together when the children needed replacements, and being good with their clothes we usually had surplus money. I must stress one point here, we went to best shops in Brum "Horne Bro's" was one, clothes on the peg had not really arrived yet.

"Miss Drake", I can use her name after all this time, but I know she would not have minded in any case, she did wish she could have bought a few things for me, but she found out how she could help, when she had a decent balance

MEMORIES OF 84 YEARS

I have been reading with interest your Bygone Birmingham. I am 84 years of age and have many memories of my early days in Deritend where I was born. Enclosed is a schoolroom photograph - me in the necklace (one from back) - taken when I was about six and I remember clearly my teacher Miss Benbow. On one occasion whilst going to school I dropped my lunch in the tram lines and quickly picked it up before the next tram came along.

I was one of 8 children and times were very hard. I remember our small house in Alcester Street having to share a bed with my brothers and sisters with coats to keep us warm as blankets were scarce. In the kitchen there was a huge coal fire on which the Sunday joint was cooked and all us kids took a turn at basting it.

I recall my brother of four years putting on my father's cap back to front and thinking he was Jackie Coughan. Outings were few but a trip to the Highgate Picture House was a real treat to watch the silent films, how I looked forward to Saturday mornings taking my one penny to get in.

I remember the drover coming up the street taking the cattle to slaughter and my brother Charlie finding a stick to "help" thus making him late for school.

Simple things we did, but many happy memories.

Mrs Annie Chadwick,
4 Windsor Road,
Castle Bromwich,
Birmingham

Lizzie's Sister "Annie's" memories [1992]
of Deritend and her days at Allcock Street School

63

Visiting Annie at her Bournemouth Training Home
Left to Right

Ada	Annie	Lizzie
. . Lizzie's best friend . .	. . aged 15 years . .	. . aged 19 years . .

over we got new bed clothes for the children's bed, how nice that was after poor old Gran's patches. We still had candle and lamplight, but all around us Gas was coming into being, so progress was slowly coming to my "Dear Old Brum".

We did buy differently, now going out were penny packets of tea or cocoa, half a loaf and half pounds of sugar. We could go to "Marsh Grocery" shop on the corner of Oxford street in Digbeth, sugar was on show in big sacks and tea, all brands in containers on the counter. Your sugar could be weighed as you bought it, in blue bags and tea was weighed also mostly in cone shaped bags. So we are getting a bit better off, well to be truthful much better off.

I try to understand how that terrible first War produced more money, we had no sign of it before, and we must not forget this was a very powerful "Empire". We sang songs at school telling us how Great we were ruling the Waves, and boys of the "Bull Dog Breed" all British Born. I don't know how it as all vanished, but of course the World is now a very small place, and we can visit countries that were so far away and some even unheard of. Back to the War and money, people wanted more of it, they worked hard and earned it during the conflict, and was this the beginning of the love for money, it does seem that way.

Well I suppose I should get along with the changing life a bit more quickly in dear Old Brum and elsewere. I sometimes think on looking back, that in between the two terrible wars, life seemed a bit more on an even keel, we had masses of unemployment all around the country, but the Midlands had a little more to offer in choice of jobs I reckon, and plenty of folks came in to search for work. We seem to have had better Summers and real hard Winters at this time, but I wonder, when you are young most things seem so different. We still cook by the fire, light the lamps, and roll mats by the doors to keep out draughts, no need to keep out burglars like today, we are all very poor but do respect our wonderful policeman and law and order. We seem to have so many shortcomings judging by today's standards regarding homes, foods and many more worldly goods. But if you look at the number of people still alive at my age, could it have had a lot going for it we have not got today, much more natural maybe, but I am certain no one will ever beat Nature.

Well my family, I seem to be straying quite a bit I had better get myself sorted out and get home. When Annie and Charlie leave school, I have to let them go, the Board of Guardians put them into jobs, with a view to their future. My sister goes to train as a children's nurse at a home for unmarried mothers in Bournemouth, for two years, it did not come easy for her, a very quiet gentle little girl, but I could do nothing about it, and the sea air did put colour into her cheeks. My friend Ada and I did visit as often as we could afford the train fare, and she did make a very good friend down there. But Charlie was pushed around quite a bit trying to fix him into a job, garden nurseries at Hatton and several more besides, but we coped and got by.

When Annie finished her training, she came back to Brum, and was placed as under-children's nurse, to the "Martineau" family, a well known respected family in the City. She was quite happy for two years in this position, and the family were very kind to her. She then moved on to the Glazier family, and strangely enough as just got a call from "Elizabeth" with birthday greeting, because she was Eighty One yesterday, and Elizabeth never forgets, and often pays a visit to my sister's humble home, such is real breeding.

Dear old Gran and myself are still jogging along, kindly neighbours are still around caring for each other, because I suppose we really were like a Clan at this time, and my friend Ada always on call if needed. Well I came home to lunch one day, I could run from Floodgate St., and see if all was well with Gran. But as usual things were never dull for me, and it seems Gran had slipped down going to get something for my lunch, but she did struggle home and waited for me. She was in great pain and my only chance of help was to get the policeman off his point duty at the bottom of the street. This was a real shame because he would have gone off duty at two o'clock, but you see things were so different then, and nothing laid on so easy as today, you could not just dial 999 in those days. My policeman came, saw poor Old Gran's distress and got an Ambulance. We went to Dudley Rd. Hospital, and after a while Gran was admitted with a fractured thigh.

The policeman and myself got out of the hospital, late in the afternoon, left to make our own ways home. This was by means of a Tram Car, and I attracted much attention because I had poor Gran's clothing just rolled up under my arm, clean and old fashioned, but I suppose it looked like I'd been shop lifting. This could have been around nineteen twenty four, and I just wondered, what next around the corner, surely better things must start happening soon. Gran came out of hospital after a while but went to stay in Bearwood with my Aunts and was well taken care of until she was ninety six years old.

Time does not stand still and one does forget quite a few things. Well my family, still started off as just a stroll down a lane with a beginning of many years ago, and here I am with heart pangs and quite a few tears. My family grown up, and changes are coming along so quickly I hardly know how to get my words together now. We certainly did get a different standard of living between the War years, still a lot of "Out of Work" but slowly a bit more money, with better packed goods on offer. I can't give dates, but bottles of milk and wrapped bread, and coal delivered to our doors, made life a little more kind to all of us in the poorer quarters of "Dear Old Brum".

My brother came out of Marston Green and went into a kind of service, he had been learning the shoe-making trade, real shoes in those days, demanding much skill. He went to a gentleman who taught and was good to him, mostly because he was a willing pupil. The sad part of this was he only knew me, still, and had to catch up with a family he just heard of through me. "My Mom's last baby" was never lost to me and still isn't, her adopted mom and aunty used to bring her to see me, unknown to the dad, who really cherished her. I did get the Gas and a cooker put in to the old tumbling down house; but still used candles in attic and kitchen; which cost me four pounds to install.

We had a five year slum clearance plan being talked about, and an Estate Dept. opened up in Moat Row, what a contrast to "Bush House" which is what it became. I got my name down on the register very early and hoped for a new house in the very near future. I can forgo a few details, and just say we all seemed to be plodding on as the old saying said, keeping our heads above water. I think Mothers were being enlightened about large families and how to control the numbers of children, every house seemed to have. I suppose this did not please every one involved, interference in private lives, did not go down very well in those days.

A plan came about to stop over crowding, and we all had forms to fill in stating how many rooms, and number of people in the house. It would be terribly hard to do this today, but it worked well when it came about. We had always had a pride in the poorest of our dwellings, and the thought of our own little garden, bathroom etc. seemed like dreams coming true. When I look back now, this was when "Old Brum" was going to disappear for ever, and it most cases needed to. The sad part was, people parted who had been neighbours for years, and scattered to outlying estates, some happy, others not, at these really big changes. I am telling you of these things, because this is your "Brum" and mine was slipping away, just leaving me, the memories I hope you have enjoyed sharing with me.

My Annie being in service only got so much time off, but always came to see her sister, as I suppose I have always been the Mother figure, as she had only faint memories of her own parents, as does Charlie, and of course, Arthur, not at all. It was many years before the baby, my sister Peggy, knew, she had a family of her very own. She would often drop in to see me, and she had started to work in an office, and doing well as a short-hand typist. She thought I was just a friend of her Mother's, and I could not tell her differently, although I kept saying I would. Then my old neighbour, who had looked after my Mom, when she was born, said she would tell her if I did not, as I was always upset when she came to see me.

The chance came to tell my sister who I was, when she came in one day after being on her way to work, and did not feel very well. She got off the tram and said she knew I would try and help her feel better. She was not terribly poorly, it seemed it was something that had to happen. I asked her who she thought I really was, and she still thought I was a friend of her Mom's. I said Peggy, I am your sister. I can recall looking at each other, but actual words have long since faded. She was eager to learn if she had other sisters and brothers; my fountain of tears sprang to life once again, as I explained everything to her. I begged her not tell her adopted Mom at this time, as she had been so good, and I would not have her hurt, and the right moment had to come.

It was quite a performance at times getting her to meet the rest of our family, which of course the girl was most eager to do. It so happened she had got a very nice boy friend, and he came to see me, and we talked things over, I'm not quite sure how we sorted it all out, I will ask her when we next meet, which may jog our memories. The strange part of this was, when my brother Arthur came to see me, it was close to when Peggy called, but a long time before they met. Arthur had settled down to his trade, taught in the cottage homes, shoe-making, and went to work for a gentleman who owned a couple of shops, I think he had lost his only son in the War.

Well my family I do hope I have not repeated myself too often, make notes and tell me later, but please do remember, I'm not so young as when we started on this lane. I suppose I could tell of many incidents at this stage, but one would open up another, and we could go on for ever. So suffice to say, we have, Our Bill, Annie, Charlie, Arthur and Peggy, and from the beginning, I have and do love every one, they were left to me by Mom and dad, and when I look back to nineteen twenty, I see the hand of God everywhere, showing me how to deal with every situation that cropped up.

I think maybe I can reach Sunday lunch-time on Sept. 3' nineteen thirty nine, and fifty years on it is very much talked about. This is one memory I can recall and still know how sad and angry I was. I saw the lads dying in trenches, in a war to end all wars, and I wondered what had happened to the promised brave "New World". I still think that maybe on August fourth, nineteen fourteen, we had not quite closed the gates of Hell that seemed to be opening again. My three brothers were involved like all dads and sons and brothers, no escape from this one. Bill, a soldier as is dad before him, Charlie, in Air force and Arthur, in Army that really took him through the mill, even though he was never very strong. By this time they were all married, but to me still my children, and their wives did not mind.

Arthur had been ambitious and wanted his own chain of shoe repair shops, and acquired three of these, but the shame was, after six weeks, being deferred from service, he was left with one shop and his wife managed that. He went all through the War. I do "Thank God", my brothers were spared to me, but this War certainly let no one go off free.

We moved from the Town to a nice house, were we still live, and so did not get all the horrors of wholesale bombing that did follow the phoney War, as it

Nan's Brothers and one of her Sisters
Top: – Our Bill and Charlie Boy –
Bottom: – Annie and Arthur –

THE WHITE HOUSE
WASHINGTON

B
8/7

Mrs. Mary Elizabeth Houghton
C/o 113 Cedar Drive, Box 244
Carver, Massachusetts 02330

80th Birthday Congratulations
from President Reagan and Nancy
during Nan's 3rd visit to America
whilst staying with her youngest brother Arthur

Nancy and I are happy to send our congratulations
for your birthday.   We hope your special day is filled
with warmth and celebration and that you enjoy much
happiness in the year to come.

Ronald Reagan

was wrongly called. I recall streets, roads and complete districts, being wiped out by landmines and constant bombing day and night. The fields were I made my daisy chain, so long ago, was to become a burial ground for a whole factory of workers, who could not reach shelters in time. I do pray hard my family, that we will never have to undergo anything like it again. I went to work again in a foundry for the second time, on War Work, but everything ends, even wars or so we are told.

When we started this writing, candles were very much in evidence, being used to light our poor homes, they came into their own during the War very much so, when we were in the dark such a lot, apart from the bad smogs that we suffered, so much worse than just a fog. But now our humble candle as taken on glamour, and is used widely for all occasions, and not just to light up poor old houses any more. I find it hard to grasp all the changes that have taken place in my dear "Old Brum", in fact I can hardly find my "Old Brum", certainly not in the City. It is strange how things do happen and we have to take notice because they seem to be meant for us. I was reading in our "Evening Mail", never been without it after all these years and costing more than the old halfpenny, when bare footed boys ran shouting through the streets.

I'm off again getting off my subject, well a Lady had wrote a letter and sent a donation to Xmas tree fund. She had been in New Zealand for many years, but had gone to my school and still filled with memories of "Dear Old Brum". Through the kindness of the Mail we got in touch and enjoyed many letters, and you my children went out early one Sunday morning, and took many pictures of the old places, and she was so happy about it all. But sadly she as now passed away, and I must admit I miss her letters very much, she was one of the well taught Floodgate Street girls of long ago.

Well to get back to my own family, Arthur as gone to America, and it was far from an easy life for him and his family. But when I think about it, he as never had it easy, but very happy knowing how we all love him, and when he comes home, make him and his wife feel very important, which they are. I have been to America four times now, who could have imagined such a thing back in nineteen twenty, when we were hard pressed, to find a penny for a candle.

We have travelled quite a long way now, down my memory lane, and only myself knows how great are the changes that have taken place in my lifetime. I have already said my "Brum" as vanished and a new one belonging to you young ones, as been born, it does seem to be full of promise and may it have the prosperity that those old fighters of long ago wished for. I could talk about this second War but much as already been written about it, and I need to light another candle.

71

I'll conclude by saying in writing :-

" May God Bless you all

and let the light of the World

that comes from the hand of Jesus

forever shine in Peace over Dear Old Brum "

Our Nan.

....

113

seem to be full of promise and may it have the prosperity that those old fighters of long ago wished for. I could talk about this second War but much as already been written about it and I need to light another candle, I'll conclude by saying in writing "May God Bless you all and let the Light of the World that comes from the hand of Jesus forever shine in "Peace" over "Dear Old Britain"

Gur Nan

Page 113, the final page of Nan's Original Narrative

Lizzie with her three daughters 1959
Left to Right
– Eileen – Lizzie – Rita – Jean –

My Grandchildren
Our Nan. x x x

Lizzie's Brothers and Sisters in 1983
Left to Right - seated
– Lizzie – Charlie – Annie – Arthur – Peggy –
and below
Mom & Our Nan's 'Farewell Letter' – written before her narrative
– and not found until after she died –

July 14' 1958

To
my wonderful family
I want to thank
each one of you for the
love and kindness you
have all given me.
It as kept me going
through all the years
which at times had not
been easy. I hope with all
(my Heart) that your love and
concern for each other will
always last. What ever befalls
any of you my Spirit will
be watching over you and
guiding you. 'God Bless" and
Take Care Of You,
Mom & Our Nan x x x
x x x

75

Sunday School and Church (Pipes Mission?)
Floodgate Street/Fazeley Street

Medical Mission & Sunday School, Floodgate Street/River Street
attended by two of Nan's daughters

Section Three

Comments, Facts and Summary

"St. Basil's by name and it was full on Sunday morning and evening. I think we must have been more "God Fearing" in those days

'more God Fearing'

The last time I saw her dressed in smart leopard skin coat and hat, and then "Good bye". This was just one more barb in my poor old heart and it still hurts funnily enough

'heart break'

This day and age sees nearly everything is done the easy way, but have we lost interest and pride? We nearly all lived in a house that opened on to a street, so we looked on that bit outside our door as our bit of patch. Well that gave us the right to keep it clean and we did just that, swept out side everyday and buckets of water swilled also.

'pride in our bit of patch'

I dont recall medals flying around at this time and the money that goes with them very often. There were only a few for the lads from the trenches, and they ended up in pawn shops windows. (Nan is getting angry

'medals for lads in the trenches'

78

Comment, Facts
and Summary

Nan's narrative is indeed meant for her family, her many references to events and people are fully understood by them all. However for we outsiders who have had the privilege of entering Nan's world, I feel it will be helpful and interesting to fill in with comment and some facts. To this end Nan's three daughters, Eileen, Rita and Jean and their families have most kindly consented to my providing the following summary.

Mary Elizabeth Shott* was born on the 7th August 1903, at No. 5, Court 3, Allison Street (opposite Well Lane), Digbeth, the first child of Alfred and Annie Shott.

By 1907 Lizzie, as the family all called her, recalls at only 4 years of age living at 'Back of' 183 Fazeley Street, Deritend, this stood on the left hand side between River Street and Floodgate Street. It is there that she describes the ' . . . yard' of ' . . . 12 or maybe 14 houses . . . 2 wash houses and 6 lavatories . . . ' with the ' . . . large lamp in the centre . . . ' and ' . . . our lamplighter . . . grand to see him reach up and lighten our darkness . . . '.

Reference to the relevant Poor Rate Assessment books shows that the Shott family had moved from Allison Street to 'No. 1/Back' of 183 Fazeley Street by 2nd April 1906, and were still there at the corresponding Rate Assessment in April 1911. The only remaining Back-to-Back properties still standing in that area of Birmingham City centre today, are in a greatly decayed state, in part by age, and are boarded-up, five windows, doors and entries still being visable, on the corner of Floodgate Street and Fazeley Street, and one probably No. 223 fronting Fazeley Street.

Again from the Poor Rate Assessment Book of 1906, it is interesting to note that Ernie McCulloch, mentioned by Nan, was a resident of one of these very properties in the court 'Back of' No. 59 Floodgate Street, at No. 6/ back-of 63. The former **'Pipe's Mission' stands on the opposite corner, being as Nan says a factory, but still retaining a Church-Like interior particularly in the upper rooms.

*Note:- spelled SHUTT on her BIRTH CERTIFICATE
**Note:- This former 'Birmingham Free Christian Society Sunday School' has not been confirmed as 'Pipe's Mission'.

Dr. Carl Chinn has of course carried out much research on this very site, and aired his views on Local Radio. He is hopeful that the saving of this most important part of 'Nan's Old Brum' will find a place in the planned renovation of this part of Deritend, under the Millenium Fund.

Kelly's Directories have enabled me to locate the position of some of the people mentioned by Nan:-

Nurse Tucker was Mrs. Jane Tucker, Midwife, who lived at No. 17 Heath Mill Lane, this house is still standing, being the 2nd house in the terrace immediately adjacent to the rear yard of the Historic 'Old Crown'.

Frederick Armstrong, Shoeing-smith, was at No. 23, whilst Joseph William Preedy, basket-maker, lived at No. 32 Heath Mill Lane on the opposite side of the road, between the then Public Library and News Rooms, and the Railway Arch. Wheatley's the Undertakers were at 39 to 47 Heath Mill Lane adjacent to Lower trinity Street.

Wilson's, Bakehouse was at No. 107 Great Barr Street, and Nan's coke wharf stood at the Adderley Street end of Glover Street, at the junction with New Bond Street.

The Forge Tavern still stands on the corner of Fazeley Street and Great Barr Street, whilst facing it on the left-hand side of Fazeley Street where today is the forecourt of a Vehicle Body repair Company, was No's. 227/229 the site of Nan's *"Marrions Pawnshop", ' . . . with a window in Heath Mill Lane and another window in Fazeley Street . . . ', next to it at 225 Fazeley Street, was Deeley's Coffee House. The Rate Assessment Book shows that Mary Deeley, also occupied the house 'Back of' the adjacent property to No. 223 Fazeley Street. The original Back-to-Back houses facing onto Fazeley Street, extending from Floodgate Street towards Heath Mill Lane were No's. 211 to 223.

183 Fazeley Street was part of a four terrace block, 181 to 187 (with one entry to the back-court between 183/185), where today stands a disused Car-wash site on the corner of River Street and Fazeley Street, (opposite to No. 180, which still stands today) and adjacent to the end wall of the Aston Screw & Rivet Co Ltd Works. An interesting fact is that the address of this company is 183 Fazeley Street, however the door on which the number is displayed is immediately adjacent to the former Unitarian Chapel, and therefore does not relate to Nan's site further back towards River Street. The back-court of the terrace now being beneath the site of the former Crane Screw Co Ltd.

all efforts to trace "Marrion's Windows" have failed to confirm this vivid memory.

* * *

Nan's memories of walks up to the Bull Ring, along High Street and through Digbeth, brings back to life many of the old traders and customs, in and around the Old Market Hall, and the Shambles, and with the, Quote ' . . . many high class shops . . . ' she mentions Sir Smedley Crooke. Kelly's Directory identifies, Crooke and Riley, Pawnbrokers at 37/38 High Street, Bull Ring to Dale End, which I assume is the Jewellers and Pawnshop mentioned by Nan.

*Mr (as he was then) John Smedley Crooke, M.P. is reported in the Evening Dispatch and Birmingham Gazette on the 30-1-1937 at the time when he became a Magistrate, describing him thus:-

' . . . a Company Director . . . and with the exception of the period 1929/31 he has represented the Deritend division in Parliament continuously since 1922. . . . prominently associated with ex-serviceman's organisations . . . ' He was knighted in 1938, and in the Birmingham Mail dated 14-2-1945, Sir John, or 'Smedley' as he was known to his friends, announced his intention not to stand at the next General Election. It is very easy to see why Our Nan considers him worthy of mention, as this same article goes on to say, ' . . . dubbed the Serviceman's M.P. . . . unsparing in his efforts, locally and nationally on behalf of Soldiers and Sailors at the time of the 1914/18 War . . . '

' . . . At the age of 18, in 1880 he joined the Royal Warwicks, . . . ' (Our Regiment, said Nan) ' . . . serving for 4 years, and 1897 to 1905 he was with the Queen's Own Worcester Hussars . . .'. The article continues, ' . . . He was Honorary Treasurer for the Midland District of the Comrades of the Great War and Treasurer to the Unity Relief Committee, which inaugurated in Birmingham a canteen for men seeking work . . . Owing to his efforts an employment exchange grew up here, and many men found work through it'. As we have seen Our Nan was greatly concerned with the difficulties facing the men returning from that war.

The Evening Despatch of the 15-10-1951, announces the death of Sir John Smedley Crooke, Conservative M.P. 'The Good Knight of Deritend', aged 90 years at his home in Alvechurch.

Both 'Our Bill' and Annie were born at the Fazeley Street home, and Nan's recollections of those 'Boaties' and the wonderful horses remain, with the Fellows, Morton & Clayton Company name still to be seen on the Fazeley Street site. The foundry in which Alfred Shott worked, and also Lizzie, was Dalman. J. C. & Sons, Iron Founders (Chunk Foundry) in River Street just down from Fazeley Street.

*Note:- These extracts are taken from 'NEWSPAPER CUTTINGS – BIRMINGHAM BIOGRAPHY' volumes 26; 29; 33; 35; 37; 43 & 44, in the LOCAL STUDIES SECTION of the BIRMINGHAM CENTRAL REFERENCE LIBRARY

At some time after April 1911 the family move to Small Heath, possibly Anderton Road, taking ' . . . a terraced house . . . with front and back doors . . . opposite to the firm of Alldays and Onions . . .', which then stood in Sydenham Road. Their new home appears to have been just around the corner from Montgomery Street, somewhere near to the Marlborough Public House, which still stands at the junction of Mongomery Street and Anderton Road. I have been unable to trace where they were living, possibly because they moved again within a very short time.

The B.S.A. factory has also gone, and the Recreation ground as I remember it with it's Annual sports day, was very much part of Nan's Daisy fields.

The date of the move back to Deritend is not known, however the April 1913 Rate Book shows them in residence at No. 11 Alcester Street, (almost opposite to Alcester Terrace) and one of a terrace of houses, that stood between Deritend High Street and Green Street, on the right hand side of Alcester Street. In their terrace, (houses and Retail shops) No's. 8 to 15 shared a common back courtyard. Now all have been demolished, as they backed on to the now sunken site of the Peugot Car Sales Showrooms and Car Park.

Opposite, on the left hand side of Alcester Street and on the corner of Warwick Street, still stands the Spotted Dog Public House, that Well in the adjacent yard (a grim reminder of a tragic death), on Alcester Street, is now covered by a factory site.

Nan's love of Floodgate Street School is very obvious, it is still there but it's educational function has changed at least twice. Closed in 1940 it was taken over as a Roman Catholic School in 1947, and then in the 1970's by the then Hall Green Technical College. It is with Nan's philosophy however that I shall always remember her school days, not only that it was the best school in Brum, but that 'Charles Dickens and William Shakespeare went to school with me'.

St. Anne's Catholic Church stands higher up Alcester Street, beyond Bradford Street, and what an amazing description Nan gives of the adoption of her youngest sister. The subsequent adoption of another sister (at only Ten-weeks of age) who after only one short visit Lizzie never saw again, seems draconian. That all of her other surviving sisters and brothers were eventually reunited as a family unit is without doubt an outstanding tribute to the courage, determination and Faith of their Sister Lizzie.

Further along Alcester Street, over Cheapside and Moseley Street, is Highgate Park. The pushing of the 'Babby' in that old wooden push-chair, and the difficulty in negotiating the Park gate could have been part of a Dave Allen sketch, and that Park-Keeper certainly left a vivid and lasting impression in that young 10 year old's mind. Some 70 years later Nan reflects ' . . . Did I bring the handy carrier home? . . . it was not on Highgate Park ground . . . that Park-Keeper he had eyes everywhere . . . ' What a lovely memory.

Nan's feelings on the state of football in the 1980's are fascinating combined with her philosphy of the attitude of the supporters of the mid 1920's. That journey with the crowd to Birmingham City ground, with her great friend Ada, and . . . 'No trouble after the match' . . . In a similar vein Nan's consideration for other people, even in times of adversity, shines throughout. In particular her concern for the Policeman on point duty at the foot of Alcester Street, who she had to call upon at the time of her Gran's accident. ' . . . he would have gone off duty at two o'clock . . .', was her concern.

At one point Nan in passing, refers to 'Brum in it's Birthday year.' I can only think that this must be a reference made in the year 1938, triggered by her recalling the 'Centenary of Incorporation, 1838–1938, celebrations', 11th – 16th July of that year, and the Pageant of Birmingham at Aston park.

As things start to improve in the late 1930's, Nan is most grateful and eagerly looking forward to the slum clearance scheme, but again that break up of the community, ' . . . people that have been neighbours for years, . . . scattered to outlying estates . . .', saddens her.

In summing up my feelings of this, Nan's narrative, I can only say that Nan's Children, her three daughters, are themselves a very close family unit, and they exhibit exactly the same characteristics as those displayed by their Mother. How could they do otherwise?

It has been a tremendous pleasure for me to have been able to present this book, *'Nan's Book'* and to have been so warmly invited into their family unit.

As 'Mom and Our Nan' says
' . . . I must tell you everything, or nothing . . . '

Thankyou Nan for telling your family 'Everything'

Maurice W. White

Acknowledgements

Roger Airey, for the modern photographs.
Patrick Baird, and his Staff at the Local Studies Section, Central Reference
        Library.
Mr Peter Wild: Company Secretary &
Mr Tony Pratt: Assistant Company Secretary,
        of Wild Manufacturing Group Ltd; for use of the Floodgate
        Street 'Mission & Free Church articles'.
Margaret D. Bird, Administrator, St Martin's-in-the-Bull Ring.
Sheila Fowler for the access to the 'Tudor' Photograph.
Robert K. Calvert, for his kind permission of use of his painting 'Saturday
        Night in the Old Bull Ring'.
Mr & Mrs G. W. Bardell, Dr Carl Chinn, Mr Chris Hughes, Peter Leather,
Bob Marsden, Mrs E. Onslow, Malcolm Stent, Mrs L. Tudor

Also to the numerous people not mentioned above, but who kindly made
contacts on my behalf.

Bibliography

. . . Poor Rate Assessment Books: 1896 : 1906 : 1911 : 1913 : 1915 : covering Deritend and Digbeth.

. . . All newspaper extracts supplied from family Records.

. . . 'FOOTBALL AT ST. ANDREW'S'
Programme: September 7th 1921
by kind permission of the Local Studies Section
City of Birmingham Central Reference Library

. . . Ordnance Survey Map extracts:
Sheet No's.: 183 : 184 : 200 : 201 : 217 : 232
Digbeth & Deritend. O.S.1: 1250. 1889 Editions.